Collins

PRACTICE MULTIPLE CHOICE QUESTIONS

CSEC®
Biology

T0328251

**Anne
Tindale**

Since 1817

HarperCollins Publishers Ltd
The News Building
1 London Bridge Street
London SE1 9GF

First edition 2017

10 9 8 7 6 5 4 3

© HarperCollins Publishers Limited 2017

ISBN 978-0-00-819471-0

www.collins.co.uk/caribbeanschools

A catalogue record for this book is available from the British Library.

Typeset by QBS Learning
Printed and bound by Grafica Veneta S. P.A.

Author: Anne Tindale
Publisher: Elaine Higgleton
Commissioning Editor: Ben Gardiner
Managing Editor: Sarah Thomas
Project Manager: Alissa McWhinnie
Copy Editor: Rebecca Ramsden
Proofreader: Sara Hulse
Answer Checker: Julie Gorman
Artwork: QBS Learning
Cover design: Kevin Robbins and Gordon MacGilp
Production: Lauren Crisp

MIX
Paper from
responsible sources
FSC www.fsc.org **FSC™ C007454**

FSC™ is a non-profit international organisation established to promote the responsible management of the world's forests. Products carrying the FSC label are independently certified to assure consumers that they come from forests that are managed to meet the social, economic and ecological needs of present and future generations, and other controlled sources.

Find out more about HarperCollins and the environment at
www.harpercollins.co.uk/green

Contents

Download answers for free at www.collins.co.uk/caribbeanschools

Structure of the CSEC® Biology Paper 1 Examination

There are **60 questions**, known as **items**, in the Paper 1 examination and the duration of the examination is **1 ¼ hours**. The paper is worth **30%** of your final examination mark.

Approximately one-sixth of the questions in the Paper 1 examination test topics in Section A, two-thirds test topics in Section B and one-sixth test topics in Section C.

Section	*Approximate* Number of Questions
A: Living Organisms in the Environment	10
B: Life Processes and Disease	40
C: Continuity and Variation	10
Total	**60**

The questions test one profile, **knowledge and comprehension**. Questions will be presented in a variety of ways including the use of diagrams, tables, data, graphs, prose or other stimulus material.

Each question is allocated 1 mark. You will not lose a mark if a question is answered incorrectly.

Examination Tips

General strategies for answering multiple choice questions

- Read every word of each question very carefully and make sure you understand exactly what it is asking. Even if you think that the question appears simple or straight forward there may be important information you could easily omit, especially small, but very important words such as *all* or *only*.

- When faced with a question that seems unfamiliar, read it very carefully. Underline or circle the key pieces of information provided. Re-read it again if necessary to make sure you are very clear as to what it is asking and that you are not misinterpreting it.

- Each question has four options, **(A)**, **(B)**, **(C)** and **(D)**, and only one is the correct answer. Look at all the options very carefully as the differences between them may be very subtle; never stop when you come across an option you think is the one required. Cross out options that you know are incorrect for certain. There may be two options that appear very similar; identify the difference between the two so you can select the correct answer.

- You have approximately 1 ¼ minutes per question. Some questions can be answered in less than 1 minute while other questions may require longer because of the reasoning or calculation involved. Do not spend too long on any one question.

- If a question appears difficult place a mark, such as an asterisk, on your answer sheet alongside the question number and return to it when you have finished answering all the other questions. Remember to carefully remove the asterisk, or other markings, from the answer sheet using a good clean eraser as soon as you have completed the question.

- Answer every question. Marks are not deducted for incorrect answers. Therefore, it is in your best interest to make an educated guess in instances where you do not know the answer. Never leave a question unanswered.

- Always ensure that you are shading the correct question number on your answer sheet. It is very easy to make a mistake, especially if you plan on returning to skipped questions.

- Some questions may ask which of the options is NOT correct or is INCORRECT, or they may state that all options are correct EXCEPT. Pay close attention to these questions because it is easy to fail to see these key words and answer the questions incorrectly.

- When answering a question that asks which option is NOT correct, is INCORRECT or that uses the word EXCEPT, place a T or an F next to each option to indicate if it is true or false. The correct answer to the question is the one with the *F*.

- Some questions may give two or more answers that could be correct and you are asked to determine which is the BEST or MOST LIKELY. You must consider each answer very carefully before making your choice because the differences between them may be very subtle.

- When a question gives three or four answers numbered **I, II** and **III** or **I, II, III** and **IV**, one or more of these answers may be correct. You will then be given four combinations as options, for example:

  (A) I only

  (B) I and II only

  (C) II and III only

  (D) I, II and III

  Place a tick by all the answers that you think are correct before you decide on the final correct combination.

- Do not make any assumptions about your choice of options, just because two answers in succession have been **C**, it does not mean that the next one cannot be **C** as well.

- Try to leave time at the end of the examination to check over your answers, but never change an answer until you have thought about it again very carefully.

Strategies for the CSEC® Biology Paper 1

- Calculators are not allowed in the examination. When answering a question that requires you to perform a calculation, work out the answer by writing your working on the question paper before you look at the options. If you do not find your answer in the options you can then go back and recheck your working for mistakes.

- If the question requires recall of a simple fact, such as the name of a labelled structure in a diagram, a chemical substance or a process, it is better to try to work out the answer before looking at the options given. Looking at the answers first could influence your choice and you may select an incorrect answer.

- When answering a question about a labelled diagram, make sure you know exactly which structure each label line is indicating before answering.

- The multiple choice examination focuses on detail. Make sure you learn all the facts, however small, that you have been taught.

Section A: Living Organisms in the Environment
A1: An Introduction to Living Organisms

1 All living organisms display the following characteristics EXCEPT

(A) excretion   (A)

(B) breathing   (B)

(C) reproduction   (C)

(D) movement   (D)

2 Which of the following are used by scientists to classify living organisms?

    I Visible characteristics

    II Molecular structure of DNA

    III Body size

    IV Developmental patterns

(A) I and II only   (A)

(B) III and IV only   (B)

(C) I, II and IV only   (C)

(D) I, III and IV only   (D)

3 Which of the following groups consists of species that are most closely related?

(A) A family   (A)

(B) A phylum   (B)

(C) A genus   (C)

(D) A class   (D)

Items **3–4** refer to the following organisms.

W   X   Y   Z

4 The organisms could be classified using

    I number of pairs of legs

    II number of body segments

    III presence or absence of antennae

  (A) I only   Ⓐ

  (B) III only   Ⓑ

  (C) I and II only   Ⓒ

  (D) I, II and III   Ⓓ

5 Organisms W and Y are

  (A) insects   Ⓐ

  (B) crustaceans   Ⓑ

  (C) arachnids   Ⓒ

  (D) myriapods   Ⓓ

6 The following are characteristics of members of the Prokaryotae kingdom EXCEPT

  (A) they are unicellular organisms   Ⓐ

  (B) their cells have cell walls   Ⓑ

  (C) their DNA is not enclosed in a nuclear membrane   Ⓒ

  (D) they possess mitochondria   Ⓓ

Item 7 refers to the following organism.

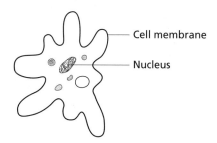

7 To which kingdom does the organism belong?

(A) Prokaryotae   Ⓐ

(B) Protoctista   Ⓑ

(C) Fungi   Ⓒ

(D) Plantae   Ⓓ

8 Which of the following pairs of phrases is correct?

	Reptiles	Amphibians	
(A)	Have a dry, waterproof skin with scales	Have a moist, non-waterproof skin with scales	Ⓐ
(B)	Lay eggs with a rubbery shell	Eggs have a hard shell	Ⓑ
(C)	Larvae develop in water	Larvae have gills for breathing	Ⓒ
(D)	Eggs are laid on land	Eggs are laid in water	Ⓓ

9 The following statements are true EXCEPT

(A) The leaves of dicotyledons are usually long and narrow.   Ⓐ

(B) The leaves of monocotyledons have parallel veins.   Ⓑ

(C) Savannah grass is a monocotyledon.   Ⓒ

(D) The seeds of the pride of Barbados plant have two cotyledons.   Ⓓ

1 The place where an organism lives is known as its

(A) niche   Ⓐ

(B) community   Ⓑ

(C) habitat   Ⓒ

(D) environment   Ⓓ

2 Which of the following terms is used to describe the role of an organism within an ecosystem?

(A) occupation   Ⓐ

(B) niche   Ⓑ

(C) vocation   Ⓒ

(D) habitat   Ⓓ

3 Abiotic environmental factors include

    I competitors

    II light intensity

    III humidity

(A) I only   Ⓐ

(B) III only   Ⓑ

(C) II and III only   Ⓒ

(D) I, II and III   Ⓓ

4 A mangrove swamp can BEST be described as

(A) a niche   Ⓐ

(B) an ecosystem   Ⓑ

(C) a community   Ⓒ

(D) an environment   Ⓓ

Item <u>5</u> refers to the following piece of apparatus.

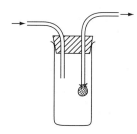

5 The apparatus is known as

(A) a pooter

(B) a specimen jar

(C) a trap

(D) a glass jar

Ⓐ

Ⓑ

Ⓒ

Ⓓ

Items <u>6–7</u> refer to the following options.

(A) a pitfall trap

(B) a plankton net

(C) a sieve

(D) a Tullgren funnel

Match EACH item below with one of the options above. Each option may be used once, more than once or not at all.

6 Is used to sample the organisms in a sample of soil.

(A)

(B)

(C)

(D)

Ⓐ

Ⓑ

Ⓒ

Ⓓ

7 Is used to sample the small invertebrates living on the ground under a tree.

(A)

(B)

(C)

(D)

Ⓐ

Ⓑ

Ⓒ

Ⓓ

8 To investigate how the vegetation in a coastal ecosystem changes with distance from the high tide mark, the BEST sampling technique would be

(A) a line transect placed across the ecosystem Ⓐ

(B) regular observation of the ecosystem Ⓑ

(C) a quadrat placed randomly within the ecosystem Ⓒ

(D) a piece of string placed across the ecosystem Ⓓ

Items **9–11** refer to the following partially completed table which gives results obtained from placing a 1 m^2 quadrat, at random, five times within an ecosystem.

Species	Number of Organisms in					Species Density	Species Frequency
	Quadrat 1	Quadrat 2	Quadrat 3	Quadrat 4	Quadrat 5		
W	0	0	16	14	2		
X	7	8	6	5	7		
Y	6	2	3	4	0		
Z	2	0	3	9	12		

9 Which species has the MOST uniform distribution throughout the ecosystem?

(A) W Ⓐ

(B) X Ⓑ

(C) Y Ⓒ

(D) Z Ⓓ

10 It would be EASIEST to calculate species density in

(A) number of organisms per cm^2 Ⓐ

(B) number of organisms per dm^2 Ⓑ

(C) number of organisms per m^2 Ⓒ

(D) number of organisms per m^3 Ⓓ

11 Which of the following statements is correct?

(A) W has the highest density. Ⓐ

(B) The species frequency of Y is 20%. Ⓑ

(C) Z has the lowest species density. Ⓒ

(D) The species frequency of X is greater than Y. Ⓓ

12 A student collected 16 millipedes from a garden and marked each with a spot of paint. She released them and, a week later, collected 20 millipedes of which 12 were marked. To the nearest whole number, the millipede population of the garden was MOST likely to be

(A) 10 Ⓐ

(B) 15 Ⓑ

(C) 26 Ⓒ

(D) 27 Ⓓ

13 Which of the following would NOT influence the distribution of a plant species?

(A) Rainfall Ⓐ

(B) Temperature Ⓑ

(C) Sources of food Ⓒ

(D) Light intensity Ⓓ

14 The size of soil particles influences

    I the pH of the soil

    II the air content of the soil

    III how easy it is for earthworms to burrow through the soil

    IV the mineral ion content of the soil

(A) I and IV only Ⓐ

(B) II and III only Ⓑ

(C) I, II and III only Ⓒ

(D) II, III and IV only Ⓓ

15 50 cm³ of water was poured into each of four separate dry soil samples of equal mass in the apparatus illustrated below. The results are given in the table below.

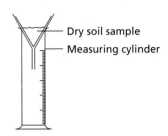

Dry soil sample
Measuring cylinder

Soil	Volume of Water Draining Through (cm³)	Time Taken for Water to Drain Through (min)	
A	17	14	Ⓐ
B	34	5	Ⓑ
C	22	11	Ⓒ
D	28	8	Ⓓ

Which soil is MOST likely to have the highest percentage of clay particles?

16 Air, present in the soil, supplies

    I earthworms with oxygen for respiration

    II hibiscus plants with carbon dioxide for photosynthesis

    III nitrogen-fixing bacteria with nitrogen to make nitrates

(A) II only   Ⓐ

(B) I and III only   Ⓑ

(C) II and III only   Ⓒ

(D) I, II and III   Ⓓ

17 Which of the following would have NO effect on aquatic organisms?

(A) Salinity   Ⓐ

(B) Humidity   Ⓑ

(C) Light intensity   Ⓒ

(D) Temperature   Ⓓ

18 Which of the following pairs of phrases MOST correctly summarises why light and temperature are important to living organisms?

	Light	Temperature
(A)	Synchronises flowering in plants	Affects the rate of photosynthesis in plants
(B)	Needed by plants for photosynthesis	Synchronises the dispersal of seeds in plants
(C)	Affects the rate of respiration in plants	Affects the rate of germination in seeds
(D)	Affects the rate of photosynthesis in plants	Synchronises reproduction in animals

Ⓐ Ⓑ Ⓒ Ⓓ

A3: Interrelationships Between Living Organisms

1 Which of the following correctly summarises the sequence of organisms in a food chain?

(A) primary producer ⟶ secondary consumer ⟶ tertiary consumer ⟶ primary consumer Ⓐ

(B) primary producer ⟶ primary consumer ⟶ secondary consumer ⟶ tertiary consumer Ⓑ

(C) primary consumer ⟶ primary producer ⟶ secondary consumer ⟶ tertiary consumer Ⓒ

(D) tertiary consumer ⟶ secondary consumer ⟶ primary consumer ⟶ primary producer Ⓓ

2 Which of the following statements is correct?

(A) Green plants can be omnivores. Ⓐ

(B) A tertiary consumer always feeds on a primary consumer. Ⓑ

(C) Secondary consumers are herbivores. Ⓒ

(D) Tertiary consumers are carnivores. Ⓓ

3 Mosquito larvae are known to feed on microscopic algae. In a freshwater pond, egrets were seen catching the tilapia, and it is also known that tilapia feed on mosquito larvae. The correct food chain for the organisms in the pond is

(A) microscopic algae ⟶ tilapia ⟶ mosquito larvae ⟶ egrets   (A)

(B) egrets ⟶ tilapia ⟶ mosquito larvae ⟶ microscopic algae   (B)

(C) mosquito larvae ⟶ microscopic algae ⟶ tilapia ⟶ egrets   (C)

(D) microscopic algae ⟶ mosquito larvae ⟶ tilapia ⟶ egrets   (D)

4 The table below gives the food sources of several animal species in a marine ecosystem.

Animal	Food Source(s)
Sea turtle	Jellyfish and crabs
Zooplankton	Plant plankton
Crab	Shrimp
Jellyfish	Zooplankton
Stingray	Crabs
Shrimp	Plant plankton

Which of the following statements is INCORRECT?

(A) Plant plankton are primary producers.   (A)

(B) Shrimp are primary consumers.   (B)

(C) Stingrays are secondary consumers.   (C)

(D) Sea turtles are tertiary consumers.   (D)

Items **5–6** refer to the following food web.

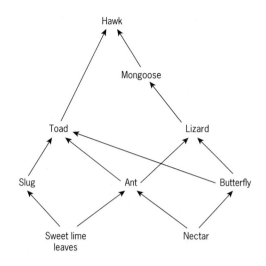

5 The primary source(s) of energy in the food web is/are

    I sweet lime leaves

    II ants

    III nectar

(A) I only   Ⓐ

(B) II only   Ⓑ

(C) I and III only   Ⓒ

(D) I, II and III   Ⓓ

6 Which of the following correctly identifies a predator and its prey?

	Predator	**Prey**	
(A)	Toad	Butterfly and slug	Ⓐ
(B)	Hawk	Mongoose and lizard	Ⓑ
(C)	Butterfly	Nectar	Ⓒ
(D)	Lizard	Ant and slug	Ⓓ

Item 7 refers to the following information.

Yeast cells were grown in a nutrient solution and a few days later a certain number of *Paramecium* were added. The graph below shows the number of yeast cells and *Paramecium* measured at regular intervals. The units on the two vertical axes are different.

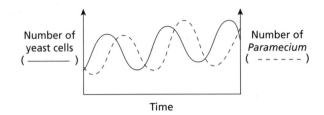

7 The two curves have similar shapes because

(A) *Paramecium* and yeast have similar life cycles   Ⓐ

(B) *Paramecium* and yeast have the same life span   Ⓑ

(C) *Paramecium* and yeast compete for the nutrients in the solution   Ⓒ

(D) *Paramecium* feeds on yeast cells   Ⓓ

8 Predator/prey relationships

I keep the numbers of organisms in ecosystems relatively constant

II can be used to control pests

III are always between a herbivore and a carnivore

(A) I only   Ⓐ

(B) III only   Ⓑ

(C) I and II only   Ⓒ

(D) I, II and III   Ⓓ

9 Decomposers are important in ecosystems because they

(A) live in the soil   Ⓐ

(B) recycle mineral nutrients   Ⓑ

(C) kill other organisms   Ⓒ

(D) make their own food   Ⓓ

10 This item refers to the following pairs of organisms

    I orchids and trees

    II ticks and cows

    III nitrogen-fixing bacteria and legumes

Which of the following correctly identifies the relationships?

	I	II	III	
(A)	Commensalism	Parasitism	Mutualism	(A)
(B)	Mutualism	Predator/prey	Parasitism	(B)
(C)	Competition	Parasitism	Mutualism	(C)
(D)	Commensalism	Predator/prey	Competition	(D)

11 In the relationship between coral polyps and green algae, the algae receive the following from the polyps EXCEPT

(A) carbon dioxide   (A)

(B) oxygen   (B)

(C) nitrogenous compounds   (C)

(D) protection   (D)

12 Parasites

    I harm their host

    II often have an intermediate host

    III gain benefit from their host

(A) I only   (A)

(B) II only   (B)

(C) I and III only   (C)

(D) I, II and III   (D)

13 Which of the following pairs of phrases correctly summarises the flow of nutrients and energy in an ecosystem?

	Nutrients	Energy	
(A)	Flow in one direction	Is recycled	Ⓐ
(B)	Flow in one direction	Flows in one direction	Ⓑ
(C)	Are recycled	Flows in one direction	Ⓒ
(D)	Are recycled	Is recycled	Ⓓ

14 Which of the following is/are the characteristic(s) of organisms at the top of a pyramid of numbers?

    I They are usually more active than those lower down

    II They are generally bigger than those lower down

    III They are more numerous than those lower down

(A) II only   Ⓐ

(B) I and III only   Ⓑ

(C) II and III only   Ⓒ

(D) I, II and III   Ⓓ

15 A food chain is given below.

mango tree ⟶ aphid ⟶ ladybird beetle ⟶ dragon fly ⟶ chameleon

Which of the following MOST accurately represents the number of organisms at each trophic level in the above food chain?

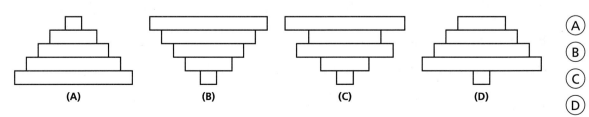

    (A)   (B)   (C)   (D)

Ⓐ Ⓑ Ⓒ Ⓓ

Item **16** refers to the following diagram which shows part of the carbon cycle.

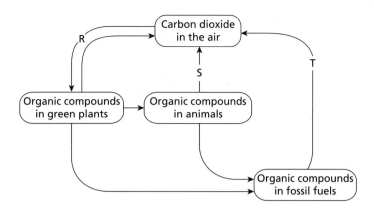

16 Which of the following correctly identifies the processes occurring at R, S and T?

	R	S	T	
(A)	photosynthesis	decomposition	respiration	Ⓐ
(B)	photosynthesis	respiration	combustion	Ⓑ
(C)	respiration	fermentation	combustion	Ⓒ
(D)	photosynthesis	respiration	decomposition	Ⓓ

17 Which of the following options correctly classifies the materials listed?

	Biodegradable	**Non-biodegradable**	
(A)	bagasse	vegetable peelings	Ⓐ
(B)	grass cuttings	synthetic fabrics	Ⓑ
(C)	plastics	copper	Ⓒ
(D)	construction rubble	manure	Ⓓ

18 The following benefits can be gained by recycling manufactured materials EXCEPT

(A) reduced availability of natural resources   Ⓐ

(B) reduced pollution   Ⓑ

(C) reduced wastage of potentially useful materials   Ⓒ

(D) reduced energy usage   Ⓓ

19 Recycling manufactured materials in Caribbean islands can be difficult because

    I there are very few different types of materials

    II it is labour and energy intensive

    III their collection, transport and storage can be problematic

(A) II only   Ⓐ

(B) I and III only   Ⓑ

(C) II and III only   Ⓒ

(D) I, II and III   Ⓓ

A4: The Impact of Humans on the Environment

1 The following are non-renewable resources EXCEPT

(A) charcoal   Ⓐ

(B) bauxite   Ⓑ

(C) petroleum   Ⓒ

(D) natural gas   Ⓓ

2 Deforestation leads to

    I loss of habitat

    II soil erosion

    III an increase in atmospheric oxygen levels

(A) I only   Ⓐ

(B) III only   Ⓑ

(C) I and II only   Ⓒ

(D) I, II and III   Ⓓ

3 The following food chain was observed in a lake where people catch trout.

water weed $\longrightarrow$ tadpoles $\longrightarrow$ trout $\longrightarrow$ heron

What would be the consequence of overfishing the lake so that the trout were almost completely eliminated?

(A) The population of tadpoles would decrease Ⓐ

(B) There would be an increase in the numbers of any other organisms that feed on tadpoles Ⓑ

(C) The quantity of waterweed would increase Ⓒ

(D) The heron population would increase Ⓓ

4 One of the MAIN consequences of pollution caused by industry is

(A) soil erosion Ⓐ

(B) improved human health Ⓑ

(C) disruption of local rainfall patterns Ⓒ

(D) changes in the balance of atmospheric gases Ⓓ

5 Which of the following is NOT a greenhouse gas?

(A) Carbon monoxide Ⓐ

(B) Carbon dioxide Ⓑ

(C) Methane Ⓒ

(D) Water vapour Ⓓ

6 Which of the following, when dissolved in rainwater, is/are the MAIN cause(s) of acid rain?

    I Sulfur dioxide

    II Carbon dioxide

    III Nitrogen dioxide

(A) I only Ⓐ

(B) II only Ⓑ

(C) I and III only Ⓒ

(D) I, II and III Ⓓ

7 Nutrient enrichment of aquatic environments leading to the growth of green algae is known as

(A) bioconcentration (A)

(B) eutrophication (B)

(C) bioaccumulation (C)

(D) phosphorylation (D)

8 A farmer constantly overuses pesticides and these make their way into a lake on his farm. Over time, which organisms are MOST likely to be harmed?

(A) Algae (A)

(B) Insect larvae (B)

(C) Small fish (C)

(D) Large fish (D)

9 Which of the following is NOT a likely consequence of burning fossil fuels in industry?

(A) A decrease in the pH of oceans (A)

(B) Blackening of plant leaves (B)

(C) A drop in sea levels (C)

(D) Lung damage (D)

10 The consequence(s) of improper disposal of garbage on the islands of the Caribbean include(s)

      I a decrease in eco-tourism

      II increased spread of disease

      III an increase in greenhouse gases being released into the atmosphere

(A) I only   Ⓐ

(B) III only   Ⓑ

(C) I and II only   Ⓒ

(D) I, II and III   Ⓓ

11 Which of the following would NOT be classified as a marine or wetland ecosystem?

(A) A fish pond   Ⓐ

(B) A coral reef   Ⓑ

(C) A mangrove swamp   Ⓒ

(D) A seagrass bed   Ⓓ

12 Marine and wetland ecosystems make a positive contribution to the economies of small island states in the following ways EXCEPT

(A) providing souvenirs for tourists   Ⓐ

(B) protecting coastlines   Ⓑ

(C) providing tourist attractions   Ⓒ

(D) supporting fishing industries   Ⓓ

13 The illegal discharge of untreated sewage into a coastal region over a period of time caused the death of most of the coral reefs directly off the coast. Residents of the area would MOST likely observe

(A) increased fish stocks   Ⓐ

(B) increased coastal erosion   Ⓑ

(C) decreased wave action   Ⓒ

(D) more sand being deposited on the beaches   Ⓓ

Item **14** refers to the following graph which shows changes in average global atmospheric carbon dioxide levels from 1960 to 2015.

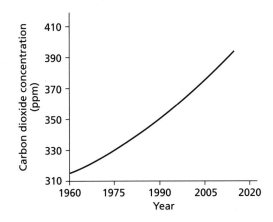

14 Which of the following will have the GREATEST impact on the small islands of the Caribbean if the trend shown in the graph continues?

(A) A rise in sea levels   (A)

(B) Changes in ecosystems   (B)

(C) More frequent wildfires   (C)

(D) Colder winters   (D)

15 Which of the following should help to reduce the rate of depletion of fossil fuels to the GREATEST extent?

(A) Re-using materials   (A)

(B) Practising reforestation   (B)

(C) Using alternative energy sources   (C)

(D) Recycling resources   (D)

16 Which of the following would be the LEAST useful strategy to employ to help conserve and restore the environment?

(A) Implementing international agreements to control pollution   (A)

(B) Increasing the use of organic farming   (B)

(C) Continually monitoring the health of ecosystems   (C)

(D) Increasing the use of fossil fuels   (D)

17 What begins to occur when the population of a particular species reaches the carrying capacity of the area it is in?

    I Overcrowding leading to competition

    II Food shortages

    III A decrease in predator numbers

    IV An increase in the spread of disease

(A) I and III only   Ⓐ

(B) II and IV only   Ⓑ

(C) I, II and III only   Ⓒ

(D) I, II and IV only   Ⓓ

18 The growth of the human population is currently at which point on the growth curve illustrated below?

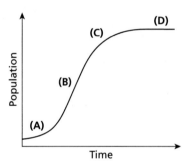

Ⓐ

Ⓑ

Ⓒ

Ⓓ

19 Which of the following is LEAST likely to lead to an increase in a country's population?

(A) Improved medical care   Ⓐ

(B) Increased emigration   Ⓑ

(C) Improved nutritional understanding   Ⓒ

(D) Improved agricultural techniques   Ⓓ

Items **1–2** refer to the following diagram of an animal cell.

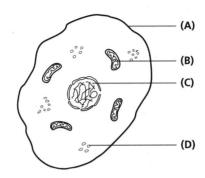

Match EACH item below with one of the options above. Each option may be used once, more than once or not at all.

1 Controls what enters and leaves the cell.

(A)   Ⓐ

(B)   Ⓑ

(C)   Ⓒ

(D)   Ⓓ

2 When removed, the cell is unable to divide.

(A)   Ⓐ

(B)   Ⓑ

(C)   Ⓒ

(D)   Ⓓ

3 Which cell type found in the human body is likely to contain most mitochondria?

(A) Red blood cell   Ⓐ

(B) Kidney cell   Ⓑ

(C) Muscle cell   Ⓒ

(D) Nerve cell   Ⓓ

4 The following comparisons are correct EXCEPT

	Mitochondria	Chloroplasts	
(A)	Rod-shaped organelles	Disc-shaped organelles	Ⓐ
(B)	Release energy	Absorb energy	Ⓑ
(C)	Do not contain a pigment	Contain chlorophyll	Ⓒ
(D)	Have no internal membranes	Have many internal membranes	Ⓓ

5 Which of the following statements is true?

(A) In a plant cell, the cell wall is composed of cellulose.   Ⓐ

(B) The cell wall of a plant cell is differentially permeable.   Ⓑ

(C) In an animal cell, the cell membrane is composed of glycogen.   Ⓒ

(D) The cell membrane of an animal cell supports the cell.   Ⓓ

6 Which of the following contain(s) genetic information?

(A) The nucleolus   Ⓐ

(B) The chromatin threads   Ⓑ

(C) The nuclear membrane   Ⓒ

(D) The nucleoplasm   Ⓓ

7 Which of the following options is INCORRECT?

	Typical Plant Cell	Typical Animal Cell	
(A)	Has a cell wall	Has no cell wall	Ⓐ
(B)	Has one large vacuole	Has many small vacuoles	Ⓑ
(C)	Contains chloroplasts	Has no chloroplasts	Ⓒ
(D)	Has no mitochondria	Contains mitochondria	Ⓓ

Items **8–9** refer to the following diagram of a bacterial cell.

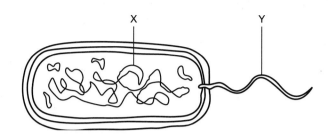

8 The correct name for structure X is

(A) nucleoid   Ⓐ

(B) nucleus   Ⓑ

(C) nucleolus   Ⓒ

(D) nucleoplasm   Ⓓ

9 Structure Y is used for

(A) reproduction   Ⓐ

(B) movement   Ⓑ

(C) support   Ⓒ

(D) anchorage   Ⓓ

10 Which of the following correctly summarises the levels of cellular organisation in multicellular organisms?

(A) cells ⟶ organs ⟶ tissues ⟶ organ systems   Ⓐ

(B) cells ⟶ tissues ⟶ organ systems ⟶ organs   Ⓑ

(C) cells ⟶ organ systems ⟶ organs ⟶ tissues   Ⓒ

(D) cells ⟶ tissues ⟶ organs ⟶ organ systems   Ⓓ

11 Which of the following would NOT be found in humans?

(A) Nerve tissue   Ⓐ

(B) Connective tissue   Ⓑ

(C) Ground tissue   Ⓒ

(D) Epithelial tissue   Ⓓ

12 A leaf of a plant is

(A) an organ   Ⓐ

(B) a tissue   Ⓑ

(C) an organ system   Ⓒ

(D) an organism   Ⓓ

13 Which of the following transport(s) water and minerals around living organisms?

    I Adipose tissue

    II Vascular tissue

    III Blood tissue

(A) III only   Ⓐ

(B) I and III only   Ⓑ

(C) II and III only   Ⓒ

(D) I, II and III   Ⓓ

14 Diffusion is important to living organisms to

    I obtain oxygen for respiration

    II get rid of carbon dioxide produced in photosynthesis

    III obtain water for photosynthesis

(A) I only   Ⓐ

(B) I and III only   Ⓑ

(C) II and III only   Ⓒ

(D) I, II and III   Ⓓ

15 Which of the following statements correctly defines osmosis?

(A) The movement of water from a weak solution to a strong solution. Ⓐ

(B) The movement of solute molecules through a differentially permeable membrane from a dilute solution to a concentrated solution. Ⓑ

(C) The movement of water molecules from a solution containing a lot of water molecules to a solution containing fewer water molecules. Ⓒ

(D) The movement of water molecules from a dilute solution to a concentrated solution through a differentially permeable membrane. Ⓓ

16

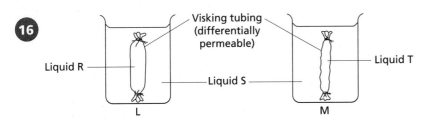

An experiment was set up as illustrated above. After 30 minutes, the Visking tubing in L had become firm and hard, and the tubing in M had collapsed. Which of the following could be the possible identities of liquids R, S and T?

	R	S	T	
(A)	Water	10% Sucrose solution	20% Sucrose solution	Ⓐ
(B)	10% Sucrose solution	20% Sucrose solution	Water	Ⓑ
(C)	20% Sucrose solution	Water	10% Sucrose solution	Ⓒ
(D)	20% Sucrose solution	10% Sucrose solution	Water	Ⓓ

Items **17–18** refer to the following diagram showing a plant cell after it was placed in Solution P.

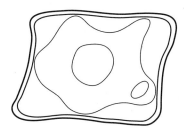

17 What deduction can be made about Solution P?

   (A) P is more dilute than the cytoplasm and cell sap of the cell.   Ⓐ

   (B) P is more concentrated than the cytoplasm and cell sap of the cell.   Ⓑ

   (C) P is a sucrose solution.   Ⓒ

   (D) P contains more water than the cytoplasm of the cell.   Ⓓ

18 Which of the following BEST describes the condition of the cell?

   (A) Flaccid   Ⓐ

   (B) Turgid   Ⓑ

   (C) Plasmolysed   Ⓒ

   (D) Wilted   Ⓓ

19 Which of the following pairs of phrases correctly summarises the importance of osmosis and active transport in living organisms?

	Osmosis	**Active Transport**	
(A)	Helps non-woody stems stand erect	Means by which leaves absorb oxygen	Ⓐ
(B)	Helps leaves obtain water for photosynthesis	Means by which roots of plants absorb mineral ions	Ⓑ
(C)	Means by which water passes out of stomata of leaves	Helps absorb glucose in the ileum	Ⓒ
(D)	Helps control water loss from leaves	Means by which carbon dioxide moves out of cells	Ⓓ

1 An organism which digests dead organic matter outside its body is known as a

(A) parasite   Ⓐ

(B) saprophyte   Ⓑ

(C) autotroph   Ⓒ

(D) saprophobe   Ⓓ

2 The raw materials needed for photosynthesis include

     I water

     II chlorophyll

     III carbon dioxide

(A) I only   Ⓐ

(B) II only   Ⓑ

(C) I and III only   Ⓒ

(D) I, II and III   Ⓓ

3 Which of the following equations MOST accurately summarises the process of photosynthesis?

(A) $CO_2 + H_2O \xrightarrow{\text{heat energy}} C_6H_{12}O_6 + O_2$ Ⓐ

(B) $6CO_2 + 6H_2O \longrightarrow C_6H_{12}O_6 + 6O_2$ Ⓑ

(C) $6CO_2 + 6H_2O \xrightarrow{\text{heat energy}} C_{12}H_{22}O_{11} + 6O_2$ Ⓒ

(D) $6CO_2 + 6H_2O \xrightarrow{\text{heat energy}} C_6H_{12}O_6 + 6O_2$ Ⓓ

4 Which of the following statements about photosynthesis is INCORRECT?

(A) The dark stage can take place in the light.   Ⓐ

(B) The oxygen produced comes from the water.   Ⓑ

(C) Chlorophyll absorbs energy during the light stage.

(D) Temperature affects both the light and dark stages.

Items **5–6** refer to the experiment illustrated below.

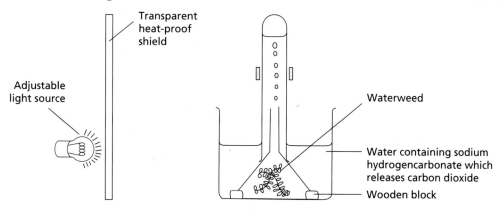

5 The MOST likely aim of the experiment is

    (A) to study the effect of light intensity on the rate of photosynthesis   (A)

    (B) to study the effect of temperature on the rate of photosynthesis   (B)

    (C) to study the effect of carbon dioxide concentration on the rate of photosynthesis   (C)

    (D) to study the effect of light intensity on the rate of respiration   (D)

6 The gas in the bubbles is MOST likely to be

    (A) nitrogen   (A)

    (B) hydrogen   (B)

    (C) oxygen   (C)

    (D) carbon dioxide   (D)

7 Which reagent would be the BEST to use to test a hibiscus leaf to see if it has been photosynthesising?

    (A) Benedict's solution   (A)

    (B) Biuret solution   (B)

    (C) Ethanol   (C)

    (D) Iodine solution   (D)

8 Which of the following would be of LEAST value to a leaf when photosynthesising?

(A) Having a thick lamina (A)

(B) Having a broad lamina (B)

(C) Lying at 90° to the sunlight (C)

(D) Having a flat lamina (D)

Items **9–10** refer to the following diagram which shows a section through a dicotyledonous leaf.

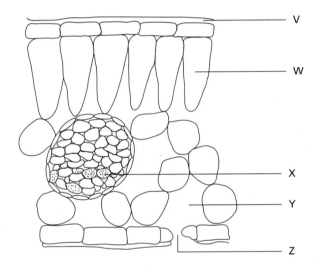

9 Structure Y is

(A) an intracellular air space (A)

(B) an intercellular air space (B)

(C) an interstellar air space (C)

(D) a pore (D)

10 Which of the following statements is INCORRECT?

(A) V prevents water from evaporating out of the leaf. (A)

(B) Most photosynthesis occurs in W. (B)

(C) X transports water to the leaf. (C)

(D) Z allows gases to diffuse in and out of the leaf. (D)

Item **11** refers to the following graph showing the effect of carbon dioxide concentration on the rate of photosynthesis.

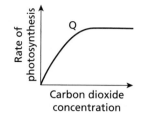

11 Which statement is the MOST accurate?

(A) As carbon dioxide concentration increases, the rate of photosynthesis increases.　　　　　　　　　　　　　　　　　　　　　　　Ⓐ

(B) Carbon dioxide concentration limits the rate of photosynthesis.　　Ⓑ

(C) Carbon dioxide concentration is the limiting factor up to point Q.　Ⓒ

(D) At point Q temperature starts to limit the rate of photosynthesis.　Ⓓ

12 Glucose, produced in photosynthesis, can be

    I converted to amino acids by leaf cells and used in growth

    II used by root cells in respiration

    III condensed to sucrose and stored in leaf cells

(A) I only　　　　　　　　　　　　　　　　　　　　　　　　　　Ⓐ

(B) I and II only　　　　　　　　　　　　　　　　　　　　　　　Ⓑ

(C) II and III only　　　　　　　　　　　　　　　　　　　　　　Ⓒ

(D) I, II and III　　　　　　　　　　　　　　　　　　　　　　　Ⓓ

13 Which element, required by all organisms, is NOT normally obtained by plants from the soil?

(A) carbon　　　　　　　　　　　　　　　　　　　　　　　　　Ⓐ

(B) hydrogen　　　　　　　　　　　　　　　　　　　　　　　　Ⓑ

(C) sulfur　　　　　　　　　　　　　　　　　　　　　　　　　Ⓒ

(D) nitrogen　　　　　　　　　　　　　　　　　　　　　　　　Ⓓ

14 A plant growing in a soil deficient in nitrogen is MOST likely to have

(A) yellow, well-developed leaves   Ⓐ

(B) dull, purplish-green, underdeveloped leaves   Ⓑ

(C) mottled leaves with yellow-brown edges which die prematurely   Ⓒ

(D) yellow, underdeveloped leaves   Ⓓ

15 Three food items, Q, R and S, were each crushed with about 2 cm^3 of water and tested with the reagents shown in the table below.

Test Solution	Resultant Colour		
	Q	**R**	**S**
Benedict's solution	Orange	Blue	Blue
Biuret solution	Purple	Purple	Blue
Iodine solution	Orange-brown	Orange-brown	Blue-black

Which of the following statements is correct?

(A) Q contained reducing sugars and starch.   Ⓐ

(B) R was the only substance which contained protein.   Ⓑ

(C) R contained reducing sugars as well as protein.   Ⓒ

(D) S contained starch only.   Ⓓ

16 Which of the following statements about enzymes is INCORRECT?

(A) Enzymes are catalysts.   Ⓐ

(B) Enzymes increase the rate of a chemical reaction.   Ⓑ

(C) Enzymes are not present at the end of a reaction.   Ⓒ

(D) Enzymes are specific.   Ⓓ

Item 17 refers to the following experiment which was set up to investigate the action of catalase enzyme found in the liver.

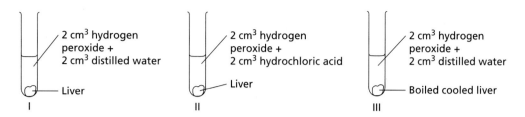

17 In which tube(s) would effervescence be seen?

(A) I only

(B) I and II only

(C) II and III only

(D) I, II and III

18 The following table shows the times taken for the enzyme amylase to break down a fixed mass of starch at different temperatures.

Temperature (°C)	Time Taken for Starch to be Broken Down (min)
10	15
25	10
35	5
45	15

What deduction can be made from these results?

(A) Temperature increases the rate at which starch is broken down.

(B) As temperature increases, the rate of amylase activity increases to a certain temperature and then decreases.

(C) As temperature increases, the rate at which starch is broken down decreases up to a certain temperature and then increases.

(D) High temperatures denature enzymes.

1 Teeth are important in the process of digestion because they

    I turn insoluble food molecules into soluble food molecules

    II break down large food molecules to smaller molecules

    III increase the surface area of pieces of food

(A) I only

(B) III only

(C) II and III only

(D) I, II and III

2 Four different types of teeth are shown below. Which plays the LEAST significant role in digestion in humans?

 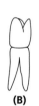  

    (A)   (B)   (C)   (D)

<u>Item **3**</u> refers to the following section through a tooth.

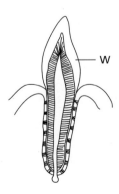

3 Which of the following would NOT help W in its role of protecting the tooth?

(A) It covers the crown of the tooth.

(B) It is extremely hard.

(C) It can be dissolved by acid in the mouth.

(D) It is relatively easy to clean.

Items **4–6** refer to the following diagram of the alimentary canal.

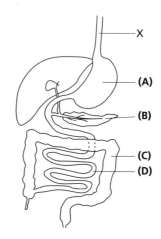

Match items 4 and 5 below with one of the parts labelled A, B, C or D in the diagram. Each part may be used once, more than once or not at all.

4 Its contents have a pH of between 1 and 2.

(A)   Ⓐ

(B)   Ⓑ

(C)   Ⓒ

(D)   Ⓓ

5 Where digestion is completed.

(A)   Ⓐ

(B)   Ⓑ

(C)   Ⓒ

(D)   Ⓓ

6 By what process does food move through structure X?

(A) Swallowing   Ⓐ

(B) Peristalsis   Ⓑ

(C) Plasmolysis   Ⓒ

(D) Translocation   Ⓓ

7 People who have their gall bladders removed are MOST likely to have to avoid eating

(A) mangoes

(B) fried bacon

(C) boiled potatoes

(D) lettuce

8 Which enzyme is responsible for completing the digestion of proteins?

(A) Erepsin (peptidase)   Ⓐ

(B) Pepsin   Ⓑ

(C) Amylase   Ⓒ

(D) Trypsin   Ⓓ

9 Which of the following is MOST likely to be deficient in a person who has difficulty digesting the sugar found in milk?

(A) Sucrase   Ⓐ

(B) Maltase   Ⓑ

(C) Pancreatic lipase   Ⓒ

(D) Lactase   Ⓓ

10 Which of the following is/are of LITTLE help in efficiently absorbing digested food in the ileum?

(A) Circular muscles in the ileum walls   Ⓐ

(B) A network of blood capillaries inside each villus Ⓑ

(C) Microvilli   Ⓒ

(D) The ileum being about 5 m long   Ⓓ

Item **11** refers to the following diagram of a villus.

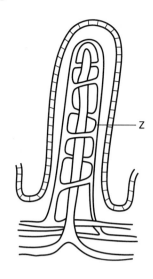

Z

11 Which of the following substances are absorbed into Z?

(A) monosaccharides, fatty acids, amino acids and vitamin D   Ⓐ

(B) starch, amino acids, minerals and vitamin C   Ⓑ

(C) monosaccharides, amino acids, minerals and vitamin C   Ⓒ

(D) glucose, protein, fatty acids and vitamin B   Ⓓ

12 A certain diet contains equal masses of glucose, starch, protein and fat. If each substance is fully oxidised, most energy would be released from

(A) glucose   Ⓐ

(B) starch   Ⓑ

(C) protein   Ⓒ

(D) fat   Ⓓ

13 It is important that a diet contains sufficient protein for the following reasons EXCEPT

(A) growth   Ⓐ

(B) to make enzymes   Ⓑ

(B) antibody production   Ⓑ

(D) storage   Ⓓ

Items **14–15** refer to the following table which shows the constituents of four foods, A, B, C and D, of equal mass.

Food	Carbohydrate (g)	Fat (g)	Protein (g)	Calcium (mg)	Vitamin C (mg)
A	5	32	21	450	–
B	45	2	15	10	95
C	24	95	5	150	5
D	15	4	60	85	15

14 Which food would be MOST suitable for a person whose bones have become weak and brittle?

(A)　　　　　　　　　　　　　　　　　　　　　　　　　　　Ⓐ

(B)　　　　　　　　　　　　　　　　　　　　　　　　　　　Ⓑ

(C)　　　　　　　　　　　　　　　　　　　　　　　　　　　Ⓒ

(D)　　　　　　　　　　　　　　　　　　　　　　　　　　　Ⓓ

15 Which food would be LEAST suitable for a person with obesity?

(A)　　　　　　　　　　　　　　　　　　　　　　　　　　　Ⓐ

(B)　　　　　　　　　　　　　　　　　　　　　　　　　　　Ⓑ

(C)　　　　　　　　　　　　　　　　　　　　　　　　　　　Ⓒ

(D)　　　　　　　　　　　　　　　　　　　　　　　　　　　Ⓓ

16 The waste product of the deamination of amino acids in the liver is

(A) glycogen　　　　　　　　　　　　　　　　　　　　　　Ⓐ

(B) urea　　　　　　　　　　　　　　　　　　　　　　　　Ⓑ

(C) fat　　　　　　　　　　　　　　　　　　　　　　　　　Ⓒ

(D) glucose　　　　　　　　　　　　　　　　　　　　　　Ⓓ

17 Which of the following is/are important in regulating blood glucose levels?

      I Insulin

      II Glycogen

      III Glucagon

(A) I only   Ⓐ

(B) I and III only   Ⓑ

(C) II and III only   Ⓒ

(D) I, II and III   Ⓓ

18 The table below gives the energy requirements of four people. Two of these people are office workers of different genders and one is a manual labourer. Which person is MOST likely to be the male office worker?

	Person	Age (years)	Energy Requirement (kJ per day)	
(A)	A	12	7500	Ⓐ
(B)	B	25	8500	Ⓑ
(C)	C	25	10 000	Ⓒ
(D)	D	25	12 500	Ⓓ

19 A vegetarian diet has which of the following advantage(s)?

      I It requires careful planning

      II It is high in dietary fibre

      III It is low in saturated fats

(A) I only   Ⓐ

(B) II only   Ⓑ

(C) II and III only   Ⓒ

(D) I, II and III   Ⓓ

20 Which of the following dietary recommendations would be BEST for a person with hypertension?

	Increased Consumption of	**Decreased Consumption of**	
(A)	Wholegrains	Fresh fruits and vegetables	Ⓐ
(B)	Fresh fruits and vegetables	Fried foods	Ⓑ
(C)	Salted fish and meat	Fatty meats	Ⓒ
(D)	Fried foods	Fish and lean meat	Ⓓ

B4: Respiration

1 Which of the following BEST describes respiration?

(A) The oxidation of glucose to produce energy   Ⓐ

(B) The use of energy by body cells   Ⓑ

(C) The release of energy from food   Ⓒ

(D) The synthesis of energy from food   Ⓓ

2 The following equation summarises the process of aerobic respiration.

$$Z + 6O_2 \longrightarrow 6CO_2 + 6H_2O + energy$$

The correct formula for Z is

(A) $C_3H_6O_3$ Ⓐ

(B) $C_6H_{12}O_6$ Ⓑ

(C) $C_{12}H_{22}O_{11}$ Ⓒ

(D) $(C_{12}H_{10}O_5)_n$ Ⓓ

3 Which of the following is/are advantages of storing energy in ATP?

    I Energy can be released where needed in a cell

    II Wastage of energy is prevented

    III Energy release is rapid

(A) I only   Ⓐ

(B) III only   Ⓑ

(C) I and II only   Ⓒ

(D) I, II and III   Ⓓ

4 In general, many more organisms respire aerobically than anaerobically because

(A) aerobic respiration is a faster process   Ⓐ

(B) aerobic respiration releases more energy per molecule of substrate than anaerobic respiration   Ⓑ

(C) most environments have a plentiful supply of oxygen   Ⓒ

(D) the products of aerobic respiration are harmless to the organisms   Ⓓ

5 Which of the following comparisons is INCORRECT?

	Aerobic Respiration	Anaerobic Respiration	
(A)	Requires oxygen	Does not require oxygen	Ⓐ
(B)	Always produces carbon dioxide and water	Always produces ethanol	Ⓑ
(C)	No energy remains in the products	At least one product contains energy	Ⓒ
(D)	Occurs in the mitochondria	Occurs in the cytoplasm	Ⓓ

6 The oxygen debt that results from strenuous exercise is repaid by breathing deeply to take in extra oxygen which is used to oxidise

(A) lactic acid   Ⓐ

(B) glycogen   Ⓑ

(C) ethanol   Ⓒ

(D) ethanoic acid   Ⓓ

Items **7–9** refer to the following diagram of the human respiratory system.

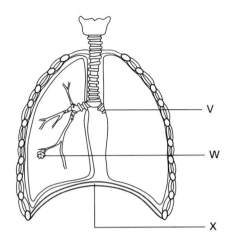

7 The structure labelled V is the

(A) oesophagus   Ⓐ

(B) trachea   Ⓑ

(C) left bronchus   Ⓒ

(D) right bronchus   Ⓓ

8 Which of the following is/are characteristics of structure W that facilitate efficient exchange of gases?

    I Their walls are made of a single layer of cells

    II Their walls are surrounded by a layer of moisture

    III They have a rich blood supply

(A) I only   Ⓐ

(B) II only   Ⓑ

(C) I and III only   Ⓒ

(D) I, II and III   Ⓓ

9 When X contracts it causes air to flow

    (A) into the lungs because air pressure in the thoracic cavity is decreased   (A)

    (B) into the lungs because air pressure in the thoracic cavity is increased   (B)

    (C) out of the lungs because air pressure in the thoracic cavity is decreased   (C)

    (D) out of the lungs because air pressure in the thoracic cavity is increased   (D)

Item **10** refers to the graph below which shows changes in air pressure inside the lungs during a complete cycle of breathing. Atmospheric pressure is 760 mm of mercury (760 mm Hg).

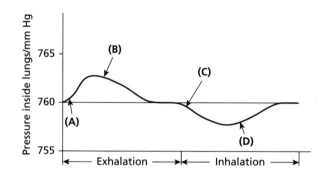

10 Which position on the graph corresponds to the point at which the ribs are beginning to be raised?

    (A)   (A)

    (B)   (B)

    (C)   (C)

    (D)   (D)

11 Which option correctly summarises the pathway of air during inhalation?

    (A) trachea, bronchioles, bronchi, alveoli   (A)

    (B) trachea, bronchi, bronchioles, alveoli   (B)

    (C) bronchi, trachea, bronchioles, alveoli   (C)

    (D) alveoli, bronchioles, bronchi, trachea   (D)

12 Inhaled air contains

    (A) less carbon dioxide than exhaled air   (A)

    (B) less oxygen than exhaled air   (B)

    (C) more carbon dioxide than exhaled air   (C)

    (D) more nitrogen than exhaled air   (D)

13 Which of the following contribute(s) to creating a large surface area in the gills of a fish?

    I The long, thin shape of each lamella

    II The large number of lamellae per gill

    III The four gills at each side of the fish's head

    (A) I only   (A)

    (B) II only   (B)

    (C) I and III only   (C)

    (D) I, II and III   (D)

14 Which of the following statements about gaseous exchange in plants is correct?

    (A) Oxygen diffuses out of a leaf during the day because only photosynthesis is occurring.   (A)

    (B) No gases are being produced in a leaf at the compensation points.   (B)

    (C) Carbon dioxide diffuses out of a leaf at night because photosynthesis is occurring more slowly than respiration.   (C)

    (D) Carbon dioxide diffuses into a leaf during the day because photosynthesis is occurring at a faster rate than respiration.   (D)

Item **15** refers to an experiment which was set up as illustrated below. Each tube contains 2 cm^3 of hydrogencarbonate indicator solution.

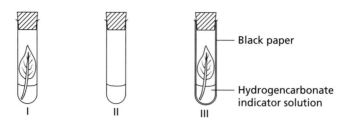

15 Which of the following would correctly summarise the colour of the indicator in each tube after 3 hours in sunlight?

	I	II	III	
(A)	Red-purple	Red-purple	Yellow-orange	Ⓐ
(B)	Red-purple	Yellow-orange	Red-purple	Ⓑ
(C)	Yellow-orange	Red-purple	Yellow-orange	Ⓒ
(D)	Yellow-orange	Yellow-orange	Red-purple	Ⓓ

16 Which of the following is LEAST likely to result from continued smoking of cigarettes?

(A) Emphysema   Ⓐ

(B) Chronic bronchitis   Ⓑ

(C) Oesophageal cancer   Ⓒ

(D) Addiction to carbon monoxide   Ⓓ

1 Multicellular organisms have developed transport systems because

    (A) they have a large surface area   Ⓐ

    (B) they have a small surface area to volume ratio   Ⓑ

    (C) their bodies are large enough to accommodate transport systems   Ⓒ

    (D) they have a large surface area to volume ratio   Ⓓ

2 Which of the following is NOT transported mainly by blood plasma?

    (A) Carbon dioxide   Ⓐ

    (B) Heat   Ⓑ

    (C) Oxygen   Ⓒ

    (D) Glucose   Ⓓ

Items **3–5** refer to the following diagram of the heart.

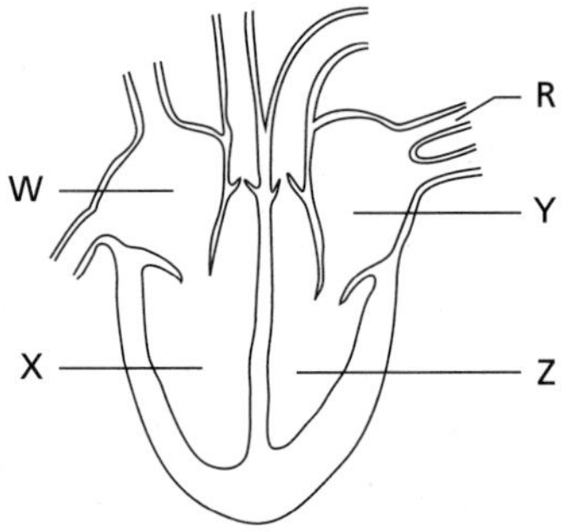

3 Chamber Y is the

    (A) right atrium   Ⓐ

    (B) right ventricle   Ⓑ

    (C) left atrium   Ⓒ

    (D) left ventricle   Ⓓ

4 The wall of chamber Z is thicker than the wall of chamber X because chamber Z has to

   (A) pump oxygenated blood   Ⓐ

   (B) withstand more pressure   Ⓑ

   (C) pump deoxygenated blood   Ⓒ

   (D) pump blood greater distances   Ⓓ

5 Blood vessel R transports blood

   (A) to the body   Ⓐ

   (B) from the body   Ⓑ

   (C) to the lungs   Ⓒ

   (D) from the lungs   Ⓓ

6 The following are directly responsible for keeping blood flowing through the heart in one direction EXCEPT

   (A) the tendons   Ⓐ

   (B) the bicuspid valve   Ⓑ

   (C) the tricuspid valve   Ⓒ

   (D) the semi-lunar valves   Ⓓ

Item **7** refers to the diagram below which shows transverse sections through three different types of blood vessels.

          L   M   N

7 Blood vessel N is

   (A) an artery   Ⓐ

   (B) a venule   Ⓑ

   (C) a capillary   Ⓒ

   (D) a vein   Ⓓ

8 Which of the following comparisons is INCORRECT?

	Arteries	Veins	
(A)	Carry low pressure blood	Carry high pressure blood	Ⓐ
(B)	Have thick walls	Have thin walls	Ⓑ
(C)	Blood flow is rapid	Blood flow is slow	Ⓒ
(D)	Blood flows in pulses	Blood flow is smooth	Ⓓ

<u>Item **9**</u> refers to the diagram below which shows two organs and their blood supply.

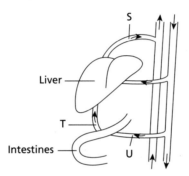

9 Which of the following correctly identifies the blood vessels S, T and U?

	S	T	U	
(A)	Hepatic portal vein	Hepatic artery	Mesenteric artery	Ⓐ
(B)	Hepatic vein	Hepatic portal vein	Mesenteric vein	Ⓑ
(C)	Hepatic artery	Hepatic vein	Mesenteric vein	Ⓒ
(D)	Hepatic vein	Hepatic portal vein	Mesenteric artery	Ⓓ

10 Through how many sets of capillaries does a red blood cell pass when circulating from the right ventricle through the brain and returning to the right ventricle?

(A) 1   Ⓐ

(B) 2   Ⓑ

(C) 3   Ⓒ

(D) 4   Ⓓ

11 The following pass through capillary walls into tissues EXCEPT

      I phagocytes

      II glucose

     III carbon dioxide

  (A) I only   Ⓐ

  (B) III only   Ⓑ

  (C) I and II only   Ⓒ

  (D) II and III only   Ⓓ

12 In what way does the blood in the renal vein differ in composition from blood in the renal artery?

  (A) It contains less urea and more carbon dioxide   Ⓐ

  (B) It contains more urea and less carbon dioxide   Ⓑ

  (C) It contains more oxygen and less urea   Ⓒ

  (D) It contains less oxygen and more urea   Ⓓ

Items **13–14** refer to the following diagram which shows a sample of cells from human blood.

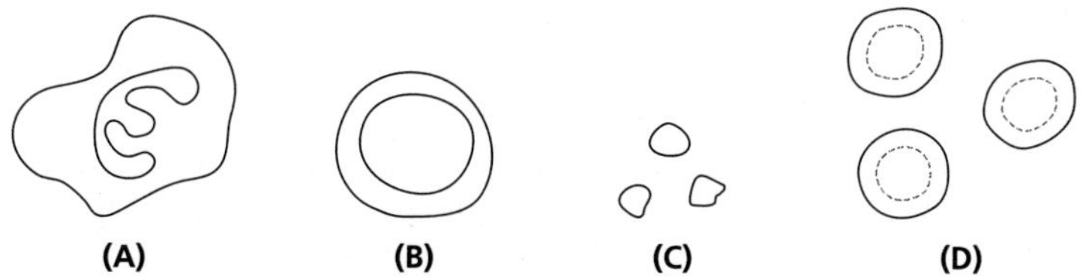

       (A)   (B)   (C)   (D)

13 Which cell is likely to ingest bacteria?

  (A)   Ⓐ

  (B)   Ⓑ

  (C)   Ⓒ

  (D)   Ⓓ

14 Which cell produces antibodies?

(A)   Ⓐ

(B)   Ⓑ

(C)   Ⓒ

(D)   Ⓓ

15 The following are characteristics of red blood cells EXCEPT

(A) they are made in red bone marrow   Ⓐ

(B) they contain haemoglobin   Ⓑ

(C) they are discus shaped   Ⓒ

(D) they are unable to reproduce   Ⓓ

16 The main function of red blood cells is to

(A) fight disease   Ⓐ

(B) transport heat to body cells   Ⓑ

(C) carry carbon dioxide away from body cells   Ⓒ

(D) carry oxygen to body cells   Ⓓ

17 The following are necessary for clot formation EXCEPT

(A) vitamin A   Ⓐ

(B) calcium ions   Ⓑ

(C) fibrinogen   Ⓒ

(D) platelets   Ⓓ

18 Which of the following is/are important in developing immunity to a disease?

      I Platelets

      II Lymphocytes

      III Phagocytes

(A) I only   Ⓐ

(B) II only   Ⓑ

(C) II and III only   Ⓒ

(D) I, II and III   Ⓓ

19 Vaccines against pathogenic diseases may contain

      I whole live pathogens

      II fragments of pathogens

      III live weakened pathogens

(A) I only   Ⓐ

(B) III only   Ⓑ

(C) II and III only   Ⓒ

(D) I, II and III   Ⓓ

20 Which of the following is LEAST likely to occur when a person is vaccinated against a communicable disease?

(A) The person's lymphocytes make antibodies against the antigens.   Ⓐ

(B) The person remains healthy when an outbreak of the disease occurs.   Ⓑ

(C) The person develops lymphocyte memory cells.   Ⓒ

(D) The person develops the disease.   Ⓓ

1 Which of the following lists consists of substances that are transported around plants?

(A) oxygen, water, minerals, amino acids   Ⓐ

(B) sucrose, amino acids, water, minerals   Ⓑ

(C) carbon dioxide, water, glucose, minerals   Ⓒ

(D) amino acids, oxygen, sucrose, carbon dioxide   Ⓓ

<u>Item 2</u> refers to the diagram below which shows a transverse section and a longitudinal section through a young dicotyledon stem.

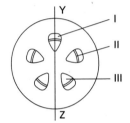 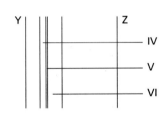

2 Which structures are responsible for transporting water?

(A) I and IV   Ⓐ

(B) II and V   Ⓑ

(C) III and IV   Ⓒ

(D) III and VI   Ⓓ

3 Which feature(s) of xylem vessels is/are important in helping them to transport water around plants?

    I They are hollow

    II They are narrow

    III They have no cross walls

(A) I only   Ⓐ

(B) I and II only   Ⓑ

(C) II and III only   Ⓒ

(D) I, II and III   Ⓓ

4 Transpiration is BEST described as

   (A) the stream of water moving from roots to leaves   Ⓐ

   (B) the movement of water through the stomata of leaves   Ⓑ

   (C) the loss of water vapour from the leaves   Ⓒ

   (D) the exchange of water vapour through the stomata of leaves   Ⓓ

5 Which of the following BEST explains how water gets from the soil to the xylem vessels of a root?

   (A) It moves into the root hairs by osmosis and moves through the cortex by active transport   Ⓐ

   (B) It moves into the root hairs by osmosis and moves through the cortex by osmosis   Ⓑ

   (C) It moves into the root hairs by active transport and moves through the cortex by diffusion   Ⓒ

   (D) It moves into the root hairs by diffusion and moves through the cortex by osmosis   Ⓓ

6 The opening and closing of stomatal pores is directly affected by

   (A) the rate of transpiration   Ⓐ

   (B) changes in turgidity of the guard cells   Ⓑ

   (C) the quantity of water in the soil   Ⓒ

   (D) the rate of respiration   Ⓓ

7   In an experiment to compare transpiration rates of the upper and lower surfaces of leaves, dry cobalt chloride paper was fixed to the leaves of three plants using Scotch tape and the average time taken for the paper to change colour completely was recorded in the table below.

Plant	Time Taken on the Upper Surface (min)	Time Taken on the Lower Surface (min)
R	7	2
S	9	5
T	13	3

What conclusion can be drawn from the results?

(A) Transpiration takes place through stomata.   Ⓐ

(B) The leaves have more stomata on their lower surfaces than their upper surfaces.   Ⓑ

(C) The rate of transpiration of the upper surfaces of the leaves is faster than   Ⓒ
the lower surfaces.

(D) The rate of transpiration of the lower surfaces of the leaves is faster than   Ⓓ
the upper surfaces.

8   The table below gives the conditions surrounding four leaves of the same species.

	Air Temperature (°C)	Relative Humidity of the Atmosphere (%)
W	25	90
X	25	70
Y	32	30
Z	32	50

If the relative humidity inside each leaf is 100%, which of the following is MOST likely to represent their rates of transpiration from the fastest to the slowest?

(A) Y, Z, X, W   Ⓐ

(B) Z, Y, W, X   Ⓑ

(C) W, X, Z, Y   Ⓒ

(D) X, W, Y, Z   Ⓓ

9 Transpiration is important to plants for the following reasons EXCEPT

    (A) it draws food up to the leaves for growth   Ⓐ

    (B) it cools plants   Ⓑ

    (C) it draws water up to the leaves for photosynthesis   Ⓒ

    (D) it helps to keep plant cells turgid   Ⓓ

10 Which of the following would BEST enable a plant to live in dry conditions?

    (A) Needle-shapes leaves with few stomata and a thin cuticle.   Ⓐ

    (B) Broad leaves with few stomata and a thick cuticle.   Ⓑ

    (C) Narrow, succulent leaves with few stomata and a thick cuticle.   Ⓒ

    (D) Broad, succulent leaves with many stomata and a thin cuticle.   Ⓓ

11 Which of the following statements is NOT correct?

    (A) Phloem always transports dissolved food downwards.   Ⓐ

    (B) Phloem transports sugars and amino acids.   Ⓑ

    (C) Phloem sieve tube elements are controlled by companion cells.   Ⓒ

    (D) Phloem sieve tube elements contain living cytoplasm.   Ⓓ

Item **12** refers to the following diagram of a longitudinal section of a phloem sieve tube.

12 X is correctly called a

    (A) perforated plate   Ⓐ

    (B) sieve plate   Ⓑ

    (C) cross wall   Ⓒ

    (D) perforated wall   Ⓓ

13 Movement of food through a flowering plant is known as

(A) transpiration   (A)

(B) translocation   (B)

(C) transfusion   (C)

(D) diffusion   (D)

14 Which of the following is/are correct about the movement of food through a flowering plant?

   I Sugars move from sugar sources to sugar sinks.

   II Stem tubers can serve as both sugar sources and sugar sinks.

   III Fruits are sugar sinks.

(A) I only   (A)

(B) III only   (B)

(C) II and III only   (C)

(D) I, II and III   (D)

15 Plants store food

   I so they have reserves for the dry season

   II so that their seeds can germinate

   III to provide food for animals

(A) I only   (A)

(B) I and II only   (B)

(C) II and III only   (C)

(D) I, II and III   (D)

16 The main food(s) stored in animals is/are

(A) fat only   Ⓐ

(B) glycogen and protein   Ⓑ

(C) glycogen and fat   Ⓒ

(D) starch and fat   Ⓓ

B7: Excretion

1 Removal of dietary fibre from the body in faeces is NOT considered to be excretion because

(A) dietary fibre is not harmful to body cells   Ⓐ

(B) dietary fibre is not digestible   Ⓑ

(C) dietary fibre is insoluble   Ⓒ

(D) dietary fibre is not produced by the body's metabolism   Ⓓ

2 Excretion is important in living organisms because if waste products are not removed they can

(A) cause weight gain   Ⓐ

(B) damage the immune system   Ⓑ

(C) cause loss of appetite   Ⓒ

(D) be harmful to body cells   Ⓓ

3 Which of the following lists consists of excretory products in plants?

(A) oxygen, carbon dioxide, tannins, calcium oxalate   Ⓐ

(B) mineral salts, carbon dioxide, uric acid, oxygen   Ⓑ

(C) calcium oxalate, water, urea, oxygen   Ⓒ

(D) water, carbon dioxide, tannins, uric acid   Ⓓ

4 Waste products are lost from plants in the following ways EXCEPT

(A) diffusion   Ⓐ

(B) leaf fall   Ⓑ

(C) active transport   Ⓒ

(D) bark loss   Ⓓ

5 Which of the following are excretory organs in animals?

    I The ileum

    II The skin

    III The lungs

    IV The spleen

(A) I and IV only   Ⓐ

(B) II and III only   Ⓑ

(C) I, II and III only   Ⓒ

(D) II, III and IV only   Ⓓ

6 The organ(s) responsible for the formation of urea in the human body is/are

(A) the kidneys   Ⓐ

(B) the liver   Ⓑ

(C) the gall bladder   Ⓒ

(D) the skin   Ⓓ

Items **7–8** refer to the diagram below which shows the human urinary system.

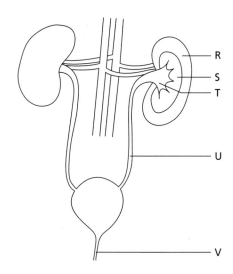

7 Which of the following correctly identifies U and V?

	U	V	
(A)	Urethra	Ureter	Ⓐ
(B)	Renal vein	Ureter	Ⓑ
(C)	Ureter	Urethra	Ⓒ
(D)	Urethra	Renal vein	Ⓓ

8 Where does ultra-filtration occur?

(A) R   Ⓐ

(B) S   Ⓑ

(C) T   Ⓒ

(D) U   Ⓓ

Items **9–10** refer to the following diagram of a kidney tubule and its blood supply.

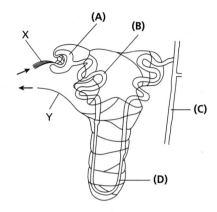

9 In which structure **(A)**, **(B)**, **(C)** or **(D)** is glucose reabsorbed into the blood?

(A)   Ⓐ

(B)   Ⓑ

(C)   Ⓒ

(D)   Ⓓ

10 In comparison to the blood in X, the blood in Y contains

(A) less urea, more glucose, less water   Ⓐ

(B) more urea, more glucose, more water   Ⓑ

(C) more urea, less glucose, more water   Ⓒ

(D) less urea, less glucose, less water   Ⓓ

11 Which of the following is/are LEAST likely to be present in the filtrate in Bowman's capsule?

(A) Amino acids   Ⓐ

(B) Sodium chloride   Ⓑ

(C) Fibrinogen   Ⓒ

(D) Vitamin C   Ⓓ

12 What must occur for glucose molecules to be reabsorbed by the blood in the kidney?

(A) Absorption of water   Ⓐ

(B) Respiration   Ⓑ

(C) An increase in the permeability of the tubule walls   Ⓒ

(D) An increase in the flow of filtrate   Ⓓ

13 Which of the following is important in osmoregulation?

(A) ADH   Ⓐ

(B) ADP   Ⓑ

(C) ATP   Ⓒ

(D) ADF   Ⓓ

14 If there is insufficient water in the blood, a person's urine will

(A) become more concentrated   Ⓐ

(B) contain a low concentration of salts   Ⓑ

(C) become very dilute   Ⓒ

(D) contain glucose   Ⓓ

15 A decrease in concentration of body fluids causes

(A) increased reabsorption of water into the blood in the kidneys   Ⓐ

(B) increased urine production   Ⓑ

(C) the walls of the second convoluted tubule to become more permeable   Ⓒ

(D) the urine to be concentrated   Ⓓ

16 If the kidneys do not function properly the body cannot

     I regulate the removal of waste

     II regulate the concentration of body fluids

     III regulate the production of waste

(A) II only   Ⓐ

(B) III only   Ⓑ

(C) I and II only   Ⓒ

(D) I, II and III   Ⓓ

B8: Movement

1 Which of the following is a correct statement about movement?

(A) Plants display both growth movements and locomotion.   Ⓐ

(B) Growth movements occur in both plants and animals.   Ⓑ

(C) During locomotion only parts of an organism move.   Ⓒ

(D) In most animals, locomotion is brought about by muscles contracting against a skeleton.   Ⓓ

2 Which of the following is a growth movement?

(A) The closing of petals of morning glory in the afternoon.   Ⓐ

(B) The closing of the trap of a Venus flytrap.   Ⓑ

(C) The bending of the stem of dumb cane (dieffenbachia) towards the light.   Ⓒ

(D) The opening of the leaves of tamarind in the morning.   Ⓓ

3 Which of the following combinations is correct?

	Part of the Axial Skeleton	Part of the Appendicular Skeleton	
(A)	Ribs	Sternum	Ⓐ
(B)	Sternum	Pelvic girdle	Ⓑ
(C)	Femur	Pectoral girdle	Ⓒ
(D)	Vertebral column	Skull	Ⓓ

4 A group of scientists discovered the skeleton of an ancient mammal. What would they look for to help them recognise the limb bones?

> **I** Projections along the length of the bones

> **II** Joints between the bones

> **III** Long, fairly thin bones

(A) I and II only   Ⓐ

(B) I and III only   Ⓑ

(C) II and III only   Ⓒ

(D) I, II and III   Ⓓ

5 Which of the following does NOT correctly match a part of the human skeleton with its function?

	Part of the Skeleton	Function	
(A)	Vertebral column	Protection	Ⓐ
(B)	Scapula	Manufacture of red blood cells	Ⓑ
(C)	Hindlimbs	Movement	Ⓒ
(D)	Ribs	Support	Ⓓ

6 The pelvic girdle

    I connects the hindlimbs to the axial skeleton

    II provides surfaces for muscle attachment

    III protects the spinal cord

(A) III only   Ⓐ

(B) I and II only   Ⓑ

(C) II and III only   Ⓒ

(D) I, II and III   Ⓓ

7 Which of the following is LEAST likely to be a reason why animals move their whole bodies from one location to another?

(A) To get exercise   Ⓐ

(B) To search for food   Ⓑ

(C) To find a mate for reproduction   Ⓒ

(D) To prevent overcrowding   Ⓓ

<u>Items **8–9**</u> refer to the following diagram of a section through a joint.

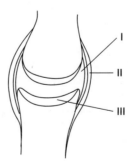

8 Which part(s) help to reduce friction in the joint?

(A) I only   Ⓐ

(B) I and III only   Ⓑ

(C) II and III only   Ⓒ

(D) I, II and III   Ⓓ

9 Which statement about the joint is NOT correct?

(A) The joint allows movement in two planes. Ⓐ

(B) The joint is a synovial joint. Ⓑ

(C) The joint is a hinge joint. Ⓒ

(D) The joint could be found at the knee. Ⓓ

10 Which statement BEST describes a ligament?

(A) It is elastic and joins bone to bone. Ⓐ

(B) It is elastic and joins muscle to bone. Ⓑ

(C) It is non-elastic and joins bone to bone. Ⓒ

(D) It is non-elastic and joins muscle to bone. Ⓓ

11 The origin of a muscle is

(A) the point where the muscle starts Ⓐ

(B) the point where the muscle ends Ⓑ

(C) the attachment point of the muscle to the bone that moves Ⓒ

(D) the attachment point of the muscle to the bone that does not move Ⓓ

Items **12–13** refer to the following simplified diagram of a human forelimb.

12 Which of the following is the extensor?

(A) R Ⓐ

(B) S Ⓑ

(C) T Ⓒ

(D) U Ⓓ

13 When attached to the human body, point Q would articulate with

(A) the pectoral girdle Ⓐ

(B) the pelvic girdle Ⓑ

(C) the collarbone Ⓒ

(D) a vertebra Ⓓ

14 Which of the following combinations is correct when the human elbow is bent?

	Biceps Muscle	Triceps Muscle	
(A)	Contracted	Contracted	Ⓐ
(B)	Contracted	Relaxed	Ⓑ
(C)	Relaxed	Contracted	Ⓒ
(D)	Relaxed	Relaxed	Ⓓ

B9: Irritability (1)

1 Which of the following statements is correct?

(A) Effectors are specialised cells which detect a stimulus. Ⓐ

(B) Receptors are muscles or glands that respond to a stimulus. Ⓑ

(C) Stimuli are changes in the internal or external environment. Ⓒ

(D) Responses are nerve impulses sent from specialised receptor cells. Ⓓ

2 Which of the following is NOT an effector in living organisms?

(A) The petiole of a leaf Ⓐ

(B) The retina of the eye Ⓑ

(C) A salivary gland Ⓒ

(D) The biceps muscle Ⓓ

3 Plants are capable of responding to

      I light

      II gravity

      III water

(A) I only   Ⓐ

(B) I and II only   Ⓑ

(C) II and III only   Ⓒ

(D) I, II and III   Ⓓ

4 An experiment was set up to investigate the responses of 20 small invertebrates. The animals were placed in the centre of two choice chambers in turn and their distribution after 20 minutes is shown below.

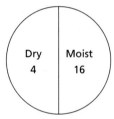 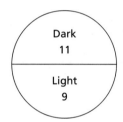

The animals were then placed in the following choice chamber.

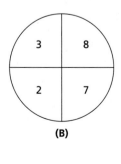

After 20 minutes, the MOST likely distribution is

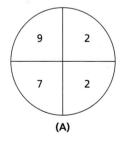 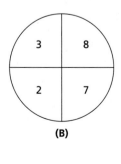 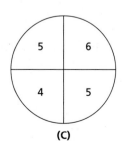 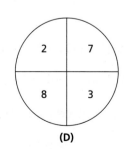

    (A)   (B)   (C)   (D)

Ⓐ Ⓑ Ⓒ Ⓓ

5 Which of the following is INCORRECT?

(A) Earthworms move away from moisture to avoid desiccation. Ⓐ

(B) Hibiscus roots grow with gravity to anchor a plant. Ⓑ

(C) Leaves of *Mimosa* fold when touched to protect them from damage. Ⓒ

(D) Woodlice move into dark places so they are hidden from predators. Ⓓ

6 The central nervous system is composed of

(A) the brain Ⓐ

(B) the spinal cord Ⓑ

(C) the brain and spinal cord Ⓒ

(D) the cerebrum, cerebellum and medulla Ⓓ

7 Sensory neurones transmit impulses from

(A) muscles to sense organs Ⓐ

(B) the brain and spinal cord to muscles Ⓑ

(C) sense organs to muscles Ⓒ

(D) sense organs to the brain and spinal cord Ⓓ

Items **8–9** refer to the following diagram of a neurone.

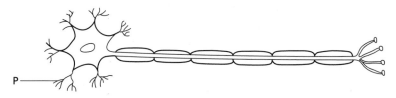

P

8 What type of neurone is illustrated?

(A) A motor neurone Ⓐ

(B) A sensory neurone Ⓑ

(C) A relay neurone Ⓒ

(D) An intermediate neurone Ⓓ

9 Structure P is

(A) an axon   (A)

(B) a fibre   (B)

(C) a dendrite   (C)

(D) a dendron   (D)

10 Which of the following is/are correct about synapses between adjacent neurones?

     I They are tiny gaps

     II They ensure impulses travel in one direction

     III Impulses pass across them by electrical means

(A) III only   (A)

(B) I and II only   (B)

(C) II and III only   (C)

(D) I, II and III   (D)

11 Which of the following is NOT a simple reflex?

(A) A dog salivating when his master says 'bone'   (A)

(B) A dog chasing a cat   (B)

(C) A dog scratching himself when bitten by a flea   (C)

(D) A dog blinking to moisten his eyes   (D)

12 In a simple reflex, in which order do nerve impulses pass through the reflex arc?

(A) receptor $\longrightarrow$ motor neurone $\longrightarrow$ relay neurone $\longrightarrow$ (A)

     sensory neurone $\longrightarrow$ effector

(B) effector $\longrightarrow$ motor neurone $\longrightarrow$ relay neurone $\longrightarrow$ (B)

     sensory neurone $\longrightarrow$ receptor

(C) effector $\longrightarrow$ sensory neurone $\longrightarrow$ relay neurone $\longrightarrow$ (C)

     motor neurone $\longrightarrow$ receptor

(D) receptor $\longrightarrow$ sensory neurone $\longrightarrow$ relay neurone $\longrightarrow$ (D)

     motor neurone $\longrightarrow$ effector

13 Which of the following does NOT correctly match a region of the central nervous system with its function?

	Region of Central Nervous System	Function	
(A)	Cerebrum	Conscious thought	Ⓐ
(B)	Cerebellum	Coordination of movement	Ⓑ
(C)	Medulla	Control of heartbeat	Ⓒ
(D)	Spinal cord	Control of balance	Ⓓ

<u>Item **14**</u> refers to the diagram of the human brain below.

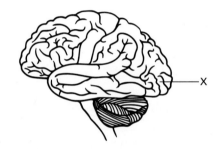

14 X is concerned with

(A) sight   Ⓐ

(B) hearing   Ⓑ

(C) speech   Ⓒ

(D) problem solving   Ⓓ

15 Which part of the body is cocaine MOST likely to affect?

(A) The skeletal muscles   Ⓐ

(B) The stomach   Ⓑ

(C) The brain   Ⓒ

(D) The lungs   Ⓓ

16 Which of the following is an INCORRECT statement?

(A) Taking drugs of any kind is illegal. Ⓐ

(B) A person can become addicted to painkillers. Ⓑ

(C) Drug abuse is a burden to society. Ⓒ

(D) Alcohol impairs normal bodily functions. Ⓓ

17 Long-term effects of alcohol abuse on the body include

    I cirrhosis of the liver

    II inflammation of the stomach walls

    III delirium tremens

(A) I only Ⓐ

(B) I and III only Ⓑ

(C) II and III only Ⓒ

(D) I, II and III Ⓓ

B10: Irritability (2)

Items **1–3** refer to the following diagram of the eye.

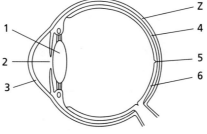

1 Z is the

(A) sclera Ⓐ

(B) choroid Ⓑ

(C) cornea Ⓒ

(D) conjunctiva Ⓓ

2 Which region contains the greatest concentration of cones?

(A) 2   Ⓐ

(B) 4   Ⓑ

(C) 5   Ⓒ

(D) 6   Ⓓ

3 Which region causes the greatest refraction of light rays?

(A) 1   Ⓐ

(B) 2   Ⓑ

(C) 3   Ⓒ

(D) 5   Ⓓ

4 The image formed on the retina of the eye is

    I inverted

    II smaller than the object

    III reversed

(A) I only   Ⓐ

(B) I and II only   Ⓑ

(C) II and III only   Ⓒ

(D) I, II and III   Ⓓ

5 Which of the following correctly identifies the events occurring when a bright light is shone into a person's eyes?

	Circular Muscles of the Iris	Radial Muscles of the Iris	Pupil	
(A)	Contract	Relax	Dilates	Ⓐ
(B)	Relax	Contract	Dilates	Ⓑ
(C)	Contract	Relax	Constricts	Ⓒ
(D)	Relax	Contract	Constricts	Ⓓ

6 What is meant by accommodation of the eye?

(A) Changing the focal length of the lens   Ⓐ

(B) Changing the size of the pupil   Ⓑ

(C) Distinguishing different light intensities   Ⓒ

(D) Judging distance   Ⓓ

7 A person is reading a book in her hand and suddenly looks up to watch an aeroplane in the sky. Which of the following correctly summarises the changes in her eyes?

	Ciliary Muscle	**Suspensory Ligaments**	**Lens**	
(A)	Relaxes	Pulled tight	Flattens	Ⓐ
(B)	Relaxes	Slacken	Bulges	Ⓑ
(C)	Contracts	Pulled tight	Flattens	Ⓒ
(D)	Contracts	Slacken	Bulges	Ⓓ

Item **8** refers to the following diagram which shows an eye with a sight defect.

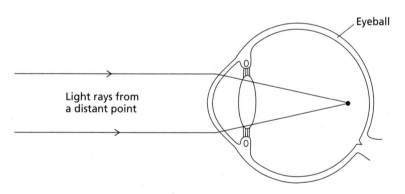

8 Which of the following statements about the defect is correct?

(A) It is caused because the lens does not bend the light rays enough.   Ⓐ

(B) It is caused by the lens being too bulged.   Ⓑ

(C) It is caused because the eyeball is too short from front to back.   Ⓒ

(D) It can be corrected by wearing converging lenses.   Ⓓ

9 Which lens, A, B, C or D would be the BEST shape to make contact lenses for a person who is suffering from long-sightedness?

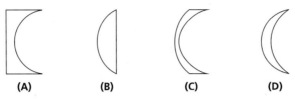

(A)   (B)   (C)   (D)

(A)
(B)
(C)
(D)

10 The graphs below show body temperature against environmental temperature. Which graph MOST accurately represents the body temperature of a mammal?

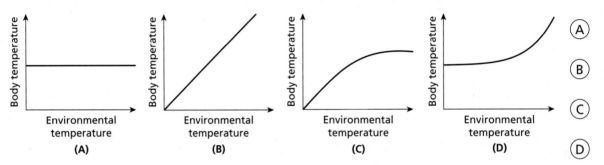

(A)
(B)
(C)
(D)

11 The MOST important function of sweat is to remove excess

(A) urea from the body

(B) heat from the body

(C) water from the body

(D) salts from the body

(A)
(B)
(C)
(D)

Items **12–13** refer to the following diagram of the human skin showing certain structures.

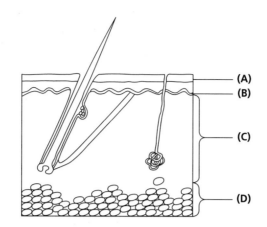

Match EACH item below with one of the options in the diagram. Each option may be used once, more than once or not at all.

12 Provides the greatest protection against the harmful rays of the Sun.

(A)   Ⓐ

(B)   Ⓑ

(C)   Ⓒ

(D)   Ⓓ

13 Is most likely to be particularly thick in polar bears.

(A)   Ⓐ

(B)   Ⓑ

(C)   Ⓒ

(D)   Ⓓ

14 Which of the following correctly summarises the events occurring in the skin when a person's core body temperature drops below 37 °C?

	Arterioles	**Hair Erector Muscles**	**Sweat Production**	
(A)	Constrict	Relax	Ceases	Ⓐ
(B)	Dilate	Contract	Occurs	Ⓑ
(C)	Constrict	Contract	Ceases	Ⓒ
(D)	Dilate	Relax	Occurs	Ⓓ

15 Which of the following statements is/are correct?

  I Good skin care helps delay the ageing process.

  II Skin should be moisturised daily.

  III Skin bleaching products are completely harmless to the skin.

(A) I only   Ⓐ

(B) I and II only   Ⓑ

(C) II and III only   Ⓒ

(C) I, II and III   Ⓒ

16 The effectiveness of sunscreen is referred to as its

(A) SFP   Ⓐ

(B) SPF   Ⓑ

(C) SRF   Ⓒ

(D) SPB   Ⓓ

Items **1–2** refer to the following information.

A scientist plants a large number of pepper seeds at the same time and considers the four methods listed below to measure the rate of growth of the seedlings.

W: Measure the length of the stems of 50 seedlings each day and calculate the daily average.

X: Count the number of leaves on each seedling each day and calculate the daily average.

Y: Dig up 10 plants each day, remove the soil from the roots, weigh them and calculate the daily average mass.

Z: Dig up 10 plants each day, remove the soil from the roots, dry them completely in an oven at 100 °C, weigh them and calculate the daily average mass.

1 Which method would be BEST to determine the growth rate of the seedlings?

(A) W   Ⓐ

(B) X   Ⓑ

(C) Y   Ⓒ

(D) Z   Ⓓ

2 What is/are the disadvantage(s) of method W?

    I It only measures one dimension of growth

    II The stems of plants are not always straight

    III It is time-consuming

(A) III only   Ⓐ

(B) I and II only   Ⓑ

(C) II and III only   Ⓒ

(D) I, II and III   Ⓓ

Items **3–4** refer to the following table which gives the number of living bacterial cells in a nutrient solution every 4 hours.

Time (h)	0	4	8	12	16	20	24	28	32	36	40
Number of Living Cells	5	8	20	60	170	320	430	490	530	550	550

3 What shape is the growth curve for the population of living cells?

(A) Sigmoid   (A)

(B) Bell-shaped   (B)

(C) A straight line at 45° to the x-axis   (C)

(D) A straight line parallel to the x-axis   (D)

4 After 40 h the number of living cells started to decrease, possibly because

    I the supply of nutrients was becoming depleted

    II waste products were accumulating

    III the large number of cells was making the solution opaque so light could not penetrate

(A) I only   (A)

(B) I and II only   (B)

(C) II and III only   (C)

(D) I, II and III   (D)

5 Cell division in stems of plants occurs in the following EXCEPT

(A) the cortex   (A)

(B) apical meristems   (B)

(C) the vascular cambium   (C)

(D) the cork cambium   (D)

6 Which of the following statements is INCORRECT?

(A) Growth in plants occurs mainly by cell division.　　　(A)

(B) Animals do not grow throughout their lifetime.　　　(B)

(C) Cell division occurs in most body tissues in animals.　　　(C)

(D) Plants usually grow throughout their lives.　　　(D)

Items **7–8** refer to the diagram of a dicotyledon seed.

Match EACH item below with one of the options above. Each option may be used once, more than once or not at all.

7 The part of the seed that will grow into the root system.

(A)　　　(A)

(B)　　　(B)

(C)　　　(C)

(D)　　　(D)

8 The place where protein is MOST likely to be stored.

(A)　　　(A)

(B)　　　(B)

(C)　　　(C)

(D)　　　(D)

9 The percentage germination of seeds is generally much lower in waterlogged soil than in non-waterlogged soil. What is the BEST conclusion that can be drawn from this?

(A) Seeds rot in waterlogged soil   Ⓐ

(B) Seeds do not germinate if water is present   Ⓑ

(C) Seeds need oxygen to germinate   Ⓒ

(D) Seeds need light for germination   Ⓓ

10 Water is necessary for germination

    I to activate enzymes to break down stored starch

    II to release energy in respiration

    III to cause the seed to swell and help burst the testa

(A) II only   Ⓐ

(B) I and III only   Ⓑ

(C) II and III only   Ⓒ

(D) I, II and III   Ⓓ

11 The straight radicle of a germinating bean seedling was marked with thin lines, equal distances apart, as shown below.

Which option below shows the MOST likely appearance of the radicle after another 3 days of growth?

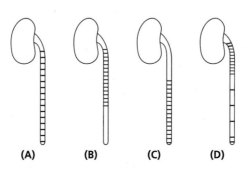

(A)   (B)   (C)   (D)

Ⓐ

Ⓑ

Ⓒ

Ⓓ

A large number of bean seeds were soaked in water overnight. Ten of the seeds were dried in an oven at 100 °C and weighed. The rest of the seeds were allowed to germinate and every day 10 were randomly selected, dried at 100 °C and weighed. The graph below shows the results.

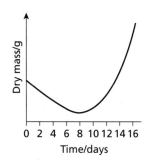

12 Which process accounts for the decrease in dry mass up to Day 8?

(A) Photosynthesis   Ⓐ

(B) Evaporation   Ⓑ

(C) Respiration   Ⓒ

(D) Dehydration   Ⓓ

13 Which process accounts for the increase in dry mass after Day 8?

(A) Cell division   Ⓐ

(B) Photosynthesis   Ⓑ

(C) Osmosis   Ⓒ

(D) Respiration   Ⓓ

1 Which of the following is the MOST important advantage of sexual reproduction over asexual reproduction?

(A) Embryos are protected during their early stages of growth   Ⓐ

(B) It produces variation among offspring   Ⓑ

(C) It ensures survival of the species   Ⓒ

(D) It produces offspring in a shorter period of time   Ⓓ

2 Asexual reproduction

     I is conservative

     II can lead to overcrowding

     III enables species to adapt to changing environmental conditions

(A) III only   Ⓐ

(B) I and II only   Ⓑ

(C) II and III only   Ⓒ

(D) I, II and III   Ⓓ

<u>Items 3–4</u> refer to the following diagram of the female reproductive system.

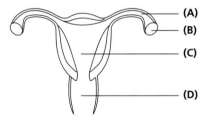

Match EACH item below with one of the options in the diagram. Each option may be used once, more than once or not at all.

3 Where fertilisation occurs.

(A)   Ⓐ

(B)   Ⓑ

(C)   Ⓒ

(D)   Ⓓ

4 Has thin walls lined with cilia.

(A)   Ⓐ

(B)   Ⓑ

(C)   Ⓒ

(D)   Ⓓ

5 The function(s) of the ovaries in humans include(s)

      I production of mature ova

      II secretion of progesterone

      III secretion of oestrogen

(A) I only   Ⓐ

(B) II only   Ⓑ

(C) I and III only   Ⓒ

(D) I, II and III   Ⓓ

Item **6** refers to the following diagram of the male reproductive system.

6 Which structure does NOT contribute to the production of semen?

(A)   Ⓐ

(B)   Ⓑ

(C)   Ⓒ

(D)   Ⓓ

7 Which of the following correctly summarises the pathway along which sperm travels?

(A) testis ⟶ sperm duct ⟶ prostate gland ⟶ urethra   Ⓐ

(B) testis ⟶ epididymis ⟶ sperm duct ⟶ ureter   Ⓑ

(C) epididymis ⟶ sperm duct ⟶ prostate gland ⟶ urethra   Ⓒ

(D) testis ⟶ epididymis ⟶ sperm duct ⟶ urethra   Ⓓ

8 The following events take place in an ovary during one complete menstrual cycle.

P: A corpus luteum develops

Q: An immature ovum undergoes meiosis

R: Ovulation

S: A Graafian follicle develops

In which order would these events occur?

(A) R, Q, S, P   Ⓐ

(B) S, Q, P, R   Ⓑ

(C) Q, R, S, P   Ⓒ

(D) Q, S, R, P   Ⓓ

9 The diagram below shows how the uterus lining changes during the menstrual cycle.

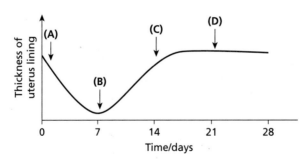

Which point indicates the state of the uterus lining when ovulation would be MOST likely to occur?

(A)   Ⓐ

(B)   Ⓑ

(C)   Ⓒ

(D)   Ⓓ

Items **10–11** refer to the following options

    (A) Oestrogen

    (B) Progesterone

    (C) Follicle stimulating hormone

    (D) Luteinising hormone

Match EACH item below with one of the options above. Each option may be used once, more than once or not at all.

10 Produced by the pituitary gland at the beginning of the menstrual cycle.

    (A)   Ⓐ

    (B)   Ⓑ

    (C)   Ⓒ

    (D)   Ⓓ

11 Stimulates the uterus lining to thicken after menstruation.

    (A)   Ⓐ

    (B)   Ⓑ

    (C)   Ⓒ

    (D)   Ⓓ

12 The fusion of sperm and ovum to form a zygote is known as

    (A) implantation   Ⓐ

    (B) ejaculation   Ⓑ

    (C) pollination   Ⓒ

    (D) fertilisation   Ⓓ

13 The following events take place between conception and birth.

T: The amnion bursts

U: The embryo sinks into the uterus lining

V: The cervix dilates

W: The placenta develops

The correct order of events is

(A) U, V, W, T   Ⓐ

(B) U, W, T, V   Ⓑ

(C) W, U, T, V   Ⓒ

(D) V, U, W, T   Ⓓ

14 Which of the following INCORRECTLY matches the structure named with its function in a developing human foetus?

	Structure	Function	
(A)	Placenta	Exchanges oxygen and carbon dioxide between mother and foetus	Ⓐ
(B)	Umbilical vein	Transports oxygen to the foetus	Ⓑ
(C)	Umbilical artery	Transports food to the foetus	Ⓒ
(D)	Amniotic fluid	Supports and protects the foetus	Ⓓ

15 Progesterone, secreted by the placenta during pregnancy,

   I inhibits ovulation during pregnancy

  II maintains a thickened uterus lining during pregnancy

 III initiates labour

(A) II only   Ⓐ

(B) I and II only   Ⓑ

(C) I and III only   Ⓒ

(D) I, II and III   Ⓓ

16 Which of the following birth control methods makes use of hormones to prevent pregnancy from occurring?

(A) Condom   Ⓐ

(B) Contraceptive pill   Ⓑ

(C) Spermicides   Ⓒ

(D) Diaphragm   Ⓓ

17 The MAIN advantage of using condoms as contraceptive devices over other contraceptives is that they

(A) are easy to use   Ⓐ

(B) are readily available   Ⓑ

(C) protect against sexually transmitted infections   Ⓒ

(D) are reliable   Ⓓ

18 Which of the following statements is INCORRECT?

(A) The spread of HIV/AIDS can be controlled by setting up immunisation programmes.   Ⓐ

(B) HIV/AIDS is caused by a virus.   Ⓑ

(C) Gonorrhoea is a bacterial infection.   Ⓒ

(D) Gonorrhoea can be treated by using antibiotics.   Ⓓ

19 The spread of gonorrhoea can be controlled by

    I using condoms during sexual intercourse

    II implementing needle and syringe exchange programmes for drug addicts

    III setting up education programmes

(A) I only   Ⓐ

(B) II only   Ⓑ

(C) I and III only   Ⓒ

(D) I, II and III   Ⓓ

20 Which of the following is NOT a possible method of transmission of HIV/AIDS?

(A) Unprotected sexual intercourse   Ⓐ

(B) Blood transfusions   Ⓑ

(C) Handling body fluids without using disposable gloves   Ⓒ

(D) Father to his unborn daughter   Ⓓ

B13: Reproduction (2)

1 Which of the following gives the correct order in which a flowering plant reproduces?

(A) fertilisation, pollination, seed formation, seed dispersal, germination   Ⓐ

(B) germination, pollination, fertilisation, seed dispersal, seed formation   Ⓑ

(C) pollination, fertilisation, seed formation, seed dispersal, germination   Ⓒ

(D) pollination, fertilisation, germination, seed formation, seed dispersal   Ⓓ

Items **2–4** refer to the following diagram of a section through a flower.

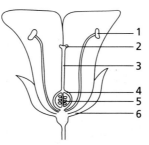

2 The structure labelled 2 is the

(A) anther   Ⓐ

(B) filament   Ⓑ

(C) stigma   Ⓒ

(D) style   Ⓓ

3 Which of the following contains a female gamete?

(A) 1   Ⓐ

(B) 3   Ⓑ

(C) 4   Ⓒ

(D) 5   Ⓓ

4 What is the main function of the structure labelled 6?

(A) To protect the flower when it was a bud   Ⓐ

(B) To protect the petals   Ⓑ

(C) To attract bees for pollination   Ⓒ

(D) To surround and support the other parts of the flower   Ⓓ

5 The MAIN function of the stamen of a flower is to

(A) produce female gametes   Ⓐ

(B) produce male gametes   Ⓑ

(C) attract insects for pollination   Ⓒ

(D) produce nectar   Ⓓ

6 Which of the following BEST describes pollination?

(A) Production of pollen grains by the anthers   Ⓐ

(B) Production of pollen grains by the stigma   Ⓑ

(C) Transfer of pollen grains from stigmas to anthers   Ⓒ

(D) Transfer of pollen grains from anthers to stigmas   Ⓓ

7 The table below compares some features of wind and insect pollinated flowers. Which option is NOT correct?

	Wind Pollinated	**Insect Pollinated**	
(A)	Pollen grains are small and smooth	Pollen grains are relatively large and spiky or sticky	Ⓐ
(B)	Petals have no scent	Petals are usually scented	Ⓑ
(C)	Stigmas project outside the flower	Stigmas are usually inside the flower	Ⓒ
(D)	Anthers are firmly attached to the filaments	Anthers are loosely attached to the filaments	Ⓓ

Item **8** refers to the following flowers.

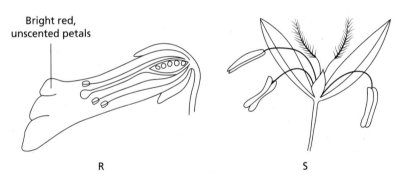

Bright red, unscented petals

R   S

8 Which option gives the MOST likely pollinating agents for the two flowers?

	Pollinating Agent		
	Flower R	**Flower S**	
(A)	Wind	Hummingbird	Ⓐ
(B)	Bat	Wind	Ⓑ
(C)	Bee	Wind	Ⓒ
(D)	Hummingbird	Bee	Ⓓ

Item **9** refers to the following diagram which shows part of a flower immediately following pollination.

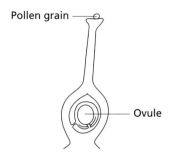

Pollen grain

Ovule

9 Which of the following BEST describes the sequence of events that follow?

(A) The pollen grain releases the male gametes which digest their way
down the style to the ovule where one fuses with the female gamete.

Ⓐ

(B) The pollen grain releases the male gametes which swim down the style
to the ovule where one fuses with the female gamete.

Ⓑ

(C) The pollen grain containing the male gametes travels down the style
to the ovule where one of the gametes fuses with the female gamete.

Ⓒ

(D) The pollen grain develops a pollen tube containing the male gametes
which grows down the style to the ovule where one gamete fuses with
the female gamete.

Ⓓ

10 The following investigation was carried out using flower buds growing on three plants
of the same species.

Plant	Treatment
X	Anthers were untouched and each bud enclosed in a paper bag
Y	Anthers were removed and each bud enclosed in a paper bag
Z	Anthers were removed and each bud left open to the air

The buds were left to open and only the flowers on plant Z produced seeds. Which
conclusion can be drawn from these results?

(A) The plant is only self pollinated   Ⓐ

(B) The plant is only cross pollinated   Ⓑ

(C) The plant is only insect pollinated   Ⓒ

(D) The plant is only wind pollinated   Ⓓ

11 Which of the following statements is NOT correct about events occurring after fertilisation in an avocado flower?

(A) The sepals remain around the fruit. Ⓐ

(B) The ovule develops into the seed. Ⓑ

(C) The integuments form the testa around the seed. Ⓒ

(D) The ovary develops into the fruit. Ⓓ

Item **12** refers to the following section through a succulent fruit.

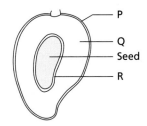

12 Which option correctly identifies P, Q and R?

	P	Q	R	
(A)	Endocarp	Mesocarp	Epicarp	Ⓐ
(B)	Epicarp	Mesocarp	Endocarp	Ⓑ
(C)	Mesocarp	Epicarp	Endocarp	Ⓒ
(D)	Epicarp	Endocarp	Mesocarp	Ⓓ

13 Seed dispersal is important to plants because

I it helps prevent the plants from becoming overcrowded

II it allows plants to colonise new habitats

III it reduces competition between the plants for light

(A) I only Ⓐ

(B) I and II only Ⓑ

(C) II and III only Ⓒ

(D) I, II and III Ⓓ

14 Which of the following BEST describes a fruit that would rely mainly on birds to disperse its seeds?

(A) Fleshy and brightly coloured with several small seeds   Ⓐ

(B) Fibrous and buoyant with one large seed   Ⓑ

(C) Succulent and brightly coloured with one large seed   Ⓒ

(D) Dry and small with a wing-like extension and one seed   Ⓓ

<u>Item 15</u> refers to the following fruits.

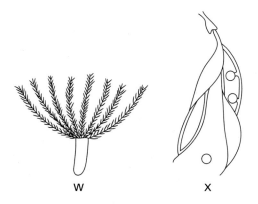

15 How are the seeds of these fruits dispersed?

	W	X	
(A)	Wind	Birds	Ⓐ
(B)	Mammals	Mechanical means	Ⓑ
(C)	Wind	Mechanical means	Ⓒ
(D)	Birds	Wind	Ⓓ

Items **1–2** refer to the following options.

(A) Deficiency disease

(B) Hereditary disease

(C) Pathogenic disease

(D) Physiological disease

Match EACH item below with one of the options above. Each option may be used once, more than once or not at all.

1 Caused by the malfunctioning of a body organ.

(A) Ⓐ

(B) Ⓑ

(C) Ⓒ

(D) Ⓓ

2 Results from a shortage or lack of a particular nutrient in the diet.

(A) Ⓐ

(B) Ⓑ

(C) Ⓒ

(D) Ⓓ

3 Which of the following statements is INCORRECT?

(A) Sickle-cell anaemia is caused by an abnormal gene passed on from   Ⓐ
one generation to the next.

(B) Hypertension is a physiological disease.   Ⓑ

(C) Scurvy is caused by a deficiency of calcium in the diet.   Ⓒ

(D) Dengue is caused by a virus.   Ⓓ

4 A new disease spread quickly through the population of a certain country. This disease was MOST likely to have been

(**A**) caused by a pathogen   Ⓐ

(**B**) inherited   Ⓑ

(**C**) caused by a poor diet   Ⓒ

(**D**) caused by drug abuse   Ⓓ

5 A vector of a disease is BEST described as

(**A**) an organism that feeds by sucking blood   Ⓐ

(**B**) an infected animal that passes a pathogenic disease on to humans   Ⓑ

(**C**) an organism that transmits pathogens from one person to another without itself being harmed   Ⓒ

(**D**) a parasite that always harms its host   Ⓓ

6 Which of the following lists consists only of diseases spread by mosquitoes?

(**A**) yellow fever, HIV/AIDS, dengue, malaria   Ⓐ

(**B**) malaria, dengue, chikungunya, yellow fever   Ⓑ

(**C**) chicken pox, influenza, dengue, chikungunya   Ⓒ

(**D**) yellow fever, malaria, dengue, influenza   Ⓓ

Items <u>7–8</u> refer to the different stages in the life cycle of a mosquito shown below.

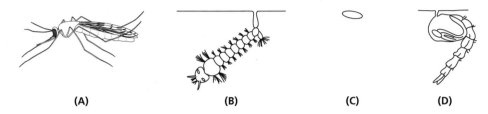

(A)　　　　　　　　(B)　　　　　　　(C)　　　　　(D)

Match EACH item below with one of the options above. Each option may be used once, more than once or not at all.

7 Which stage would NOT be found in water?

(A)　　　　　　　　　　　　　　　　　　　　　　　　Ⓐ

(B)　　　　　　　　　　　　　　　　　　　　　　　　Ⓑ

(C)　　　　　　　　　　　　　　　　　　　　　　　　Ⓒ

(D)　　　　　　　　　　　　　　　　　　　　　　　　Ⓓ

8 During which stage does the most rapid growth occur?

(A)　　　　　　　　　　　　　　　　　　　　　　　　Ⓐ

(B)　　　　　　　　　　　　　　　　　　　　　　　　Ⓑ

(C)　　　　　　　　　　　　　　　　　　　　　　　　Ⓒ

(D)　　　　　　　　　　　　　　　　　　　　　　　　Ⓓ

9 Which of the following would be LEAST effective in controlling mosquitoes?

(A) Adding insecticides to areas of standing water　　　　Ⓐ

(B) Introducing a predator of mosquitoes to breeding areas　Ⓑ

(C) Eliminating areas of standing water　　　　　　　　Ⓒ

(D) Spraying areas where adult mosquitoes are found with insecticides　Ⓓ

10 When a diabetic injects insulin into her thigh, the insulin

      I speeds up removal of blood glucose by the kidneys

      II stimulates cells of the pancreas to produce more insulin

      III stimulates body cells to absorb glucose for respiration

(A) II only   Ⓐ

(B) III only   Ⓑ

(C) I and III only   Ⓒ

(D) I, II and III   Ⓓ

11 What hormone, produced by the pancreas, has the opposite effect to insulin?

(A) Adrenalin   Ⓐ

(B) Glycogen   Ⓑ

(C) Thyroxine   Ⓒ

(D) Glucagon   Ⓓ

12 Which of the following would be LEAST effective in controlling diabetes and hypertension?

(A) Eating a balanced diet containing lots of fresh fruits and vegetables   Ⓐ

(B) Exercising moderately and regularly   Ⓑ

(C) Practising good personal hygiene   Ⓒ

(D) Attending regular check-ups with a doctor   Ⓓ

13 Which of the following would be MOST effective in controlling the spread of a viral disease?

(A) Quarantine persons with the disease   Ⓐ

(B) Treat infected individuals with antibiotics   Ⓑ

(C) Practice good sanitation   Ⓒ

(D) Prepare food using good food handling techniques   Ⓓ

14 The outbreak of a certain disease within a human population is UNLIKELY to result in

(A) loss of productivity   Ⓐ

(B) increased earnings   Ⓑ

(C) increased demands on health services   Ⓒ

(D) loss of human resources   Ⓓ

Section C: Continuity and Variation
C1: Inheritance and Variation (1)

1 The basic unit of heredity is known as

(A) a chromatid   Ⓐ

(B) a chromosome   Ⓑ

(C) a gene   Ⓒ

(D) an allele   Ⓓ

2 Which of the following is composed of a single DNA molecule wrapped around histones?

(A) A chromosome   Ⓐ

(B) An allele   Ⓑ

(C) A centriole   Ⓒ

(D) A centromere   Ⓓ

3 A horse has a diploid number of 64. What is its haploid number?

    (A) 16   Ⓐ

    (B) 32   Ⓑ

    (C) 64   Ⓒ

    (D) 128   Ⓓ

4 Which of the following statements is INCORRECT?

    (A) Cells produced by mitosis are genetically identical.   Ⓐ

    (B) Each cell produced in mitosis contains the haploid number of chromosomes.   Ⓑ

    (C) Mitosis is essential for growth.   Ⓒ

    (D) Mitosis maintains the species number of chromosomes.   Ⓓ

Item **5** refers to the following diagrams which show some of the stages of mitosis.

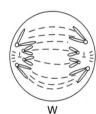 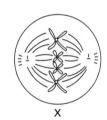  

W   X   Y   Z

5 The correct order of the stages is

    (A) Y, Z, X, W   Ⓐ

    (B) W, Y, Z, X   Ⓑ

    (C) Y, X, Z, W   Ⓒ

    (D) W, Z, X, Y   Ⓓ

6 Why is it important that chromosomes replicate during mitosis?

    (A) To ensure no genes are lost as the cell divides   Ⓐ

    (B) So that all chromosomes are passed on to the daughter cells   Ⓑ

    (C) To double the number of chromosomes that each daughter cell receives   Ⓒ

    (D) So the daughter cells each receive the same complement of chromosomes   Ⓓ

<u>Item 7</u> refers to the following diagram of the body cell of a certain animal undergoing mitosis.

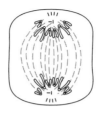

7 What is the diploid number of chromosomes per body cell?

(A) 24   Ⓐ

(B) 12   Ⓑ

(C) 6   Ⓒ

(D) 3   Ⓓ

8 A cheek cell begins to divide. How many cells would be produced after the cell has divided three times?

(A) 3   Ⓐ

(B) 8   Ⓑ

(C) 9   Ⓒ

(D) 16   Ⓓ

9 New grass plants produced asexually from a single plant would

    I have the same genetic makeup as the parent plant

    II be known as a clone

    III look identical to each other

(A) I only   Ⓐ

(B) I and II only   Ⓑ

(C) II and III only   Ⓒ

(D) I, II and III   Ⓓ

10 Which of the following is NOT an example of asexual reproduction?

(A) Hibiscus plants grown from seeds   Ⓐ

(B) New sugar cane plants growing from cuttings   Ⓑ

(C) Plantlets growing around the margins of *Bryophyllum* leaves   Ⓒ

(D) Orchids grown by tissue culture   Ⓓ

11 Farmers traditionally grow sweet potato plants from stem cuttings rather than by using sexual means because

     I it increases variation

     II it decreases the time to harvest

     III it maintains desirable characteristics

(A) I only   Ⓐ

(B) II only   Ⓑ

(C) II and III only   Ⓒ

(D) I, II and III   Ⓓ

12 Which of the following comparisons is INCORRECT?

	Mitosis	Meiosis	
(A)	Occurs in body cells except in the reproductive organs	Occurs only in the reproductive organs	Ⓐ
(B)	No exchange of genetic material occurs	Chromatids exchange genetic material	Ⓑ
(C)	Two genetically identical cells are produced	Four genetically different cells are produced	Ⓒ
(D)	Chromosomes duplicate themselves	Chromosomes do not duplicate themselves	Ⓓ

13 Why is it important that meiosis rather than mitosis occurs during gamete formation?

    I Meiosis allows gametes to be produced in a faster time

    II Meiosis produces haploid gametes in preparation for fertilisation

    III Meiosis allows twice the number of cells to be produced

(A) II only   Ⓐ

(B) I and II only   Ⓑ

(C) I and III only   Ⓒ

(D) I, II and III   Ⓓ

Item **14** refers to the following diagram which shows the nucleus of an immature ovum in an ovary before dividing.

14 Which of the following would NOT be a possible nucleus of a viable mature ovum?

Ⓐ
Ⓑ
Ⓒ
Ⓓ

  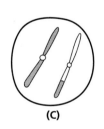 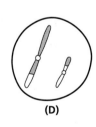

    (A)   **(B)**   **(C)**   **(D)**

15 Every gamete produced by meiosis has a different combination of genes because

      I chromatids of homologous chromosomes cross over and exchange genes

      II chromosome pairs arrange themselves randomly around the equators of the spindles

      III chromatids disintegrate and reform in random ways

(A) I only   Ⓐ

(B) I and II only   Ⓑ

(C) II and III only   Ⓒ

(D) I, II and III   Ⓓ

C2: Inheritance and Variation (2)

1 The genotype of an organism is defined as

(A) the number of chromosomes in each body cell   Ⓐ

(B) its observable characteristics   Ⓑ

(C) its type of reproduction   Ⓒ

(D) the composition of genes within its cells   Ⓓ

2 Which term refers to two or more alternative versions of a gene?

(A) Chromatids   Ⓐ

(B) Chromosomes   Ⓑ

(C) Chromatin threads   Ⓒ

(D) Alleles   Ⓓ

3 Which of the following is true about a dominant allele?

(A) It produces the same phenotype whether its paired allele is the same or different   Ⓐ

(B) It gives a greater chance of survival than a recessive allele   Ⓑ

(C) It does not undergo mutation   Ⓒ

(D) It only shows its effect on the phenotype if its paired allele is different   Ⓓ

4 Which of the following represents the genotype of a homozygous recessive individual?

(A) RR Ⓐ

(B) Rr Ⓑ

(C) rr Ⓒ

(D) r Ⓓ

5 What phenotypic ratio of offspring would be obtained when crossing two heterozygous individuals?

(A) 1 : 1 Ⓐ

(B) 2 : 1 Ⓑ

(C) 3 : 1 Ⓒ

(D) 4 : 1 Ⓓ

6 In pea plants, tall plants are dominant to dwarf plants. A tall plant, produced from crossing a tall and a dwarf plant, is crossed with a dwarf plant. If 120 seeds germinate, it would be expected that

(A) 120 are tall Ⓐ

(B) 60 are tall and 60 are dwarf Ⓑ

(C) 90 are tall and 30 are dwarf Ⓒ

(D) 120 are dwarf Ⓓ

7 In fruit flies, the allele for red eyes is dominant to the allele for purple eyes. To find out if a red-eyed fly was homozygous or heterozygous it was crossed with a purple-eyed fly. Which of the following would be the correct ratio of offspring if the red-eyed fly was homozygous?

(A) 100% purple-eyed Ⓐ

(B) 50% red-eyed and 50% purple-eyed Ⓑ

(C) 75% red-eyed and 25% purple-eyed Ⓒ

(D) 100% red-eyed Ⓓ

8 In mice, the allele for black coat is dominant to the allele for brown coat. If two black mice produce a litter of four mice which all have black coats and then produce a second litter of four which contains one brown mouse, then

(A) both parents are homozygous ⒜

(B) one parent only is homozygous ⒝

(C) both parents are heterozygous ⒞

(D) it is not possible to deduce the genotypes of the parents ⒟

Items **9–10** refer to the following family tree which shows the inheritance of albinism, a condition caused by a recessive allele, n.

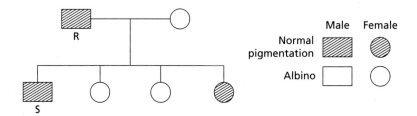

9 The genotype of individual R is

(A) NN ⒜

(B) Nn ⒝

(C) N ⒞

(D) nn ⒟

10 If person S married a heterozygous female, what would be the probability that their first-born child would have albinism?

(A) 0% ⒜

(B) 25% ⒝

(C) 50% ⒞

(D) 75% ⒟

11 A pure breeding red-flowered plant was crossed with a pure breeding white-flowered plant and all the offspring had pink flowers. If one of the pink-flowered plants was self pollinated, what would be the expected phenotypes of the offspring?

(A) All pink   Ⓐ

(B) Half red and half white   Ⓑ

(C) One-third red, one-third white and one-third pink   Ⓒ

(D) One-quarter red, one-quarter white and half pink   Ⓓ

12 A man and his wife have two children. His wife's blood group is O and his children have blood groups A and B. What is the man's genotype?

(A) $I^A I^B$ Ⓐ

(B) $I^A I^A$ Ⓑ

(C) $I^A I^O$ Ⓒ

(D) $I^B I^O$ Ⓓ

13 The genotypes of four individuals are given in the table below where Hb^A represents the allele for producing normal haemoglobin A and Hb^S represents the allele for producing abnormal haemoglobin S.

Individual	Genotype
T	Hb^AHb^A (male)
U	Hb^AHb^S (female)
V	Hb^SHb^S (female)
W	Hb^AHb^S (male)

Which of the following statements is/are correct?

I Individual T will have sickle-cell anaemia.

II Individual U will have the sickle-cell trait.

III If individuals U and W marry and have children, there is a 50% chance their first-born child will have sickle-cell anaemia.

(A) II only   Ⓐ

(B) I and III only   Ⓑ

(C) II and III only   Ⓒ

(D) I, II and III   Ⓓ

14 Which of the following correctly summarises the combination of sex chromosomes in the nuclei of human body cells?

	Male	Female	
(A)	XX	XY	Ⓐ
(B)	XY	XX	Ⓑ
(C)	YY	XX	Ⓒ
(D)	XY	YY	Ⓓ

15 Haemophilia is caused by an X-linked recessive allele. A heterozygous woman marries a man with normal blood clotting. What would be the chance of each of their sons having haemophilia?

(A) All would have haemophilia   Ⓐ

(B) 1 in 2 chance   Ⓑ

(C) 1 in 4 chance   Ⓒ

(D) No chance   Ⓓ

16 Organisms produced asexually from a single parent have

(A) identical genotypes only   Ⓐ

(B) identical phenotypes only   Ⓑ

(C) identical genotypes and phenotypes   Ⓒ

(D) different genotypes and phenotypes   Ⓓ

17 Which of the following would NOT give rise to genetic variation in living organisms?

(A) Mutation   Ⓐ

(B) Sexual reproduction   Ⓑ

(C) Meiosis   Ⓒ

(D) Light intensity   Ⓓ

18 Variation is important in living organisms because

     I it enables species to gradually change and become better adapted to their environment

     II it ensures that all individuals of a species survive in unchanging environments

     III it makes it less likely that any adverse environmental changes will wipe out an entire species

  (A) II only   Ⓐ

  (B) I and II only   Ⓑ

  (C) I and III only   Ⓒ

  (D) I, II and III   Ⓓ

19 Which of the following shows discontinuous variation?

  (A) Hand size   Ⓐ

  (B) Hair colour   Ⓑ

  (C) Tongue rolling ability   Ⓒ

  (D) Leaf size   Ⓓ

20 The heights of 50 female students of approximately the same ages were measured. Which graph MOST accurately shows the expected results of the investigation?

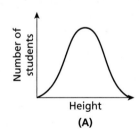 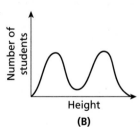 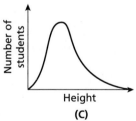 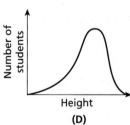

       (A)   **(B)**   **(C)**   **(D)**

1 Which of the following statements is NOT correct?

(A) Members of a species have common ancestry.   (A)

(B) Members of a species live in the same area.   (B)

(C) Members of a species closely resemble each other.   (C)

(D) Members of a species are normally capable of interbreeding to produce fertile   (D)
offspring.

2 Which of the following could possibly result in the formation of a new species?

   I A few seeds of plant X floating across the water to a different island.

   II Species Y spreading throughout an island and some of its members adapting to a different source of food.

   III A river forming a new branch which starts to flow through a forest.

(A) III only   (A)

(B) I and II only   (B)

(C) I and III only   (C)

(D) I, II and III   (D)

3 Which of the following MOST likely contributed to the extinction of the Caribbean monk seal?

   I An increase in the numbers of its prey

   II Overhunting by humans

   III Habitat loss

(A) II only   (A)

(B) I and II only   (B)

(C) I and III only   (C)

(D) I, II and III   (D)

4 The following form the basis of the theory of natural selection EXCEPT

    (A) in nature there is a constant struggle for survival   (A)

    (B) living organisms often produce more offspring than are needed to maintain their numbers   (B)

    (C) organisms best adapted to their environment are least likely to survive   (C)

    (D) all organisms show variation, much of which can be inherited   (D)

5 Mutations provide raw material for natural selection because

    (A) they increase the frequency of undesirable genes   (A)

    (B) they reduce genetic variation   (B)

    (C) they increase the number of genes   (C)

    (D) they are sudden changes in genetic material   (D)

6 Which of the following does/do NOT provide evidence for natural selection?

    I Peppered moths in Britain

    II Anole lizards of the Caribbean

    III Beef cattle in the Caribbean

    (A) I only   (A)

    (B) III only   (B)

    (C) I and II only   (C)

    (D) II and III only   (D)

7 Charles Darwin concluded that the 13 species of finches on the Galapagos Islands

    (A) had all adapted to the same food sources   (A)

    (B) probably evolved from one ancestral South American species   (B)

    (C) were identical to 13 finch species in South America   (C)

    (D) had adapted to 13 different habitats on the Islands   (D)

8 Increasing numbers of people worldwide are dying each year from bacterial infections because bacteria are becoming

   (A) immune to antibiotics   (A)

   (B) indifferent to antibiotics   (B)

   (C) resistant to antibiotics   (C)

   (D) susceptible to antibiotics   (D)

9 Which of the following is NOT a reason why humans employ artificial selection in plant and animal breeding?

   (A) To decrease genetic diversity   (A)

   (B) To increase yields   (B)

   (C) To decrease time to maturity   (C)

   (D) To increase resistance to disease   (D)

10 The process by which humans change the traits of one organism by inserting genetic material from a different organism into its DNA is known as

   (A) gene therapy   (A)

   (B) cloning   (B)

   (C) genetic engineering   (C)

   (D) artificial selection   (D)

11 Genetic engineering is being used to

      I improve crop yields

      II produce vaccines

      III protect crops against deficiency diseases

(A) I only   Ⓐ

(B) I and II only   Ⓑ

(C) II and III only   Ⓒ

(D) I, II and III   Ⓓ

12 Golden rice has been produced by genetic engineering to

(A) increase rice yields worldwide   Ⓐ

(B) increase resistance of rice plants to pests   Ⓑ

(C) decrease the use of fertilisers in rice fields   Ⓒ

(D) help fight vitamin A deficiency in developing countries   Ⓓ

13 Which was the first hormone to be produced commercially by genetic engineering?

(A) Insulin   Ⓐ

(B) Glucagon   Ⓑ

(C) Thyroxine   Ⓒ

(D) Adrenalin   Ⓓ

14 Which of the following is NOT a possible advantage of genetic engineering?

(A) Decreased resistance of crops to disease   Ⓐ

(B) Increased nutritional value of food   Ⓑ

(C) Reduced need for chemical pesticides   Ⓒ

(D) Purer and safer drugs   Ⓓ

15 Which of the following are possible disadvantages of genetic engineering?

    I Increased numbers of pesticide-resistant pests

    II Reduced use of live weakened vaccines

    III Designer babies

    IV Increased allergens in food

(A) I and III only   Ⓐ

(B) II and IV only   Ⓑ

(C) I, II and III only   Ⓒ

(D) I, III and IV only   Ⓓ

16 DNA testing can be used for the following EXCEPT

(A) to detect a genetic disorder   Ⓐ

(B) to treat a physiological disease   Ⓑ

(C) to determine paternity   Ⓒ

(D) to help solve crimes   Ⓓ